C000102623

Pouring Old Wine into New Skins?

UCITS & Asset Management in the EU after MiFID

A CEPS–ECMI Task Force Report

CHAIRMAN: **ALAIN LECLAIR**
Chairman, AFG (French Asset Management Association)

RAPPORTEURS: **KAREL LANNOO**
Chief Executive Officer &
Senior Research Fellow, CEPS

JEAN-PIERRE CASEY
Associate Research Fellow, CEPS &
Manager, Compliance Advisory, Barclays Wealth

WITH CONTRIBUTIONS FROM: **GIOVANNI CANDIGLIOTA &
ALESSANDRA CHIRICO**

CENTRE FOR EUROPEAN POLICY STUDIES
EUROPEAN CAPITAL MARKET INSTITUTE

BRUSSELS

The Centre for European Policy Studies (CEPS) is an independent policy research institute in Brussels. Its mission is to produce sound policy research leading to constructive solutions to the challenges facing Europe. As a research institute, CEPS takes no position on matters of policy. The views expressed are attributable only to the authors in a personal capacity and not to any institution with which they are associated.

The European Capital Markets Institute (ECMI) is an independent entity, which undertakes and disseminates research on European capital markets and seeks to contribute in a substantial manner to ongoing policy debates. ECMI operates under the management of CEPS.

This report is based on discussions in a joint CEPS-ECMI Task Force on Asset Management and the UCITS Review. The members of the Task Force participated in extensive debates in the course of several meetings and submitted comments on earlier drafts of this report. Its contents contain the general tone and direction of the discussion, but its recommendations do not necessarily reflect a full common position reached among all members of the Task Force, nor do they necessarily represent the views of the institutions to which the members belong. A list of participants and invited guests and speakers appears in Annex 3 at the end of this report.

The rapporteurs wish to thank the Chairman, Alain Leclair, and the members of the Task Force for their input into the discussions and their contributions to this report, and Giovanni Candigliota for research assistance.

ISBN-13: 978-92-9079-678-7

© Copyright 2008, Centre for European Policy Studies.

All rights reserved. No part of this publication may be reproduced, stored in a retrieval system or transmitted in any form or by any means – electronic, mechanical, photocopying, recording or otherwise – without the prior permission of the Centre for European Policy Studies.

Centre for European Policy Studies
Place du Congrès 1, B-1000 Brussels
Tel: (32.2) 229.39.11 Fax: (32.2) 219.41.51
E-mail: info@ceps.eu
Website: http://www.ceps.eu

CONTENTS

List of Tables

List of Figures

List of Boxes

FOREWORD

Behind the strange acronym of UCITS (Undertakings for Collective Investment in Transferable Securities) has hidden one of the most impressive success stories of financial Europe for the past two decades. Thanks to an excellent cooperation between European private stakeholders and European institutions, citizens and corporations – both within the Single Market and at the worldwide level – now have access to a unique financial instrument, which has proved its high qualities over time. Such a tool has made a significant contribution to building a strong investment fund industry in Europe, representing today more than €8 trillion in asset management and 42% of the worldwide investment fund industry. UCITS are the only investment vehicles to be offered worldwide, i.e. not only in Europe but also in South America and Asia.

But times are changing, from various perspectives.

At global level, new needs for financing are appearing or developing: infrastructure, education, health, personal retirement funds, among others. To be able to meet these fast-growing needs, public sources of financing have to be complemented. Such needs and the limits of public financing require not only developing financing by institutional investors, but also a mass financing by retail investors all over the world. What better vehicle than investment funds could capture such a large investor coverage?

Therefore, the European framework for investment funds must urgently incorporate such new needs. Until now, this framework has been limited to UCITS, for which the scope of eligible assets and management techniques is restricted (although partially extended in recent years). If both European professionals and European politicians want to ensure that Europe stays ahead of the curve, we need further flexibility in such a scope. This could be achieved either through the UCITS framework or by developing an additional European framework that would be dedicated to non-UCITS funds (covering investment funds such as funds of hedge funds, real estate funds and private equity funds, for instance). If we don't take such a political initiative at European level now, we face the risk of missing the train of innovation and many other business opportunities for the next decade.

The approach to be followed is not one in which further constraints are created through regulation but rather, on the contrary, to use regulation to facilitate and enhance access to investment funds by investors, looking in particular for diversification and safety, especially after the recent and deep financial turmoil and the need to restore confidence.

From this perspective, the best way to move forward is probably on the one hand to take advantage of the recently transposed MiFID as the UCITS is clearly the most transparent financial instrument, but also on the other hand to make sure that the product regulation is still maintained in order to guarantee its own quality and safety before any distribution.

Another major challenge regards the booming competition between the whole range of financial instruments. While the segmentation between capital market products, insurance products and investment funds was rather clear some decades ago, the lines are more and more blurred nowadays, with the possibility to wrap the same financial product within different vehicles. It appears that all over the world, including in Europe, these various series of products very often depend on separate product legislation/regulation.

Each set of product legislation/regulation has its own merits and must not be criticised as such – as for instance the global success of the UCITS was built on a product directive, i.e. the UCITS Directive.

However, we must admit that if not made entirely consistent one with the other, the variety of product legislation/regulation has often led to regulatory arbitrage in favour of the products that are the most flexible, the easiest to passport cross-border – or the cheapest for investors. From this latter perspective, regarding costs, we must applaud the huge efforts made by the European Commission services in recent years to reduce costs and to bring more flexibility for UCITS, through the desire to allow for cross-border tools, such as fund mergers or master-feeder schemes, as well as really streamlining the notification procedure and the so-called 'simplified prospectus'.

In addition, European policy-makers and regulators also have to think about the constraints faced by UCITS management companies when they want to make use of the so-called 'Management Company Passport'. The existing UCITS Directive contradicts itself on this crucial topic, preventing it from working in practice. Such an obstacle to the general principle of freedom of providing services is not only contrary to the Treaty but it also generates huge costs in practice, estimated at around €1 billion per year for European Management Companies. This lack of passport represents the last barrier to be removed in order for fund managers to be able to operate throughout the European Union. Its implementation would translate in practice into the achievement of a truly liberal European framework.

Considering the fierce competition between financial products mentioned above, introducing a real Management Company Passport – with its promise of both flexibility and lower costs – would be a great success for the European industry and ultimately for European investors.

Looking back today at the successful story of UCITS, I express the hope that the excellent cooperation between European institutions and private stakeholders will be continued, in order to push forward for a real fund Single Market and the reinforcement of a highly competitive European industry.

Alain Leclair
Chairman of the CEPS Task Force on UCITS and Asset Management
Chairman of AFG (French Asset Management Association)
April 2008, Paris

EXECUTIVE SUMMARY

The European asset management industry, and in particular the investment fund sector, has experienced tremendous growth in recent years. This growth was impressive as much in terms of the value of assets under management, the sheer number of products developed and the pace of product innovation, as it was in terms of the fundamental changes the industrial organisation of the sector has undergone, including the trend towards greater specialisation.

These very consequential changes pose challenges for regulators to respond in a constructive way. The ongoing adaptation of the regime governing Undertakings for Collective Investment in Transferable Securities (UCITS) is an attempt by regulators to update the framework governing regulated collective investment schemes to reflect these developments and to foster further market integration. Another challenge arises from the introduction of the Markets in Financial Instruments Directive (MiFID), whose direct and indirect effects on the asset management sector remain to be properly scoped out. Asset management firms will be directly impacted by MiFID rules on inducements and on conduct of business generally, particularly best execution, with attendant consequences for distribution models and execution arrangements. Because MiFID takes a lighter-touch approach than UCITS, there are serious concerns over the possible uneven playing field that may emerge by coping with both MiFID and UCITS rules: it has been argued that potentially competing non-UCITS products might be sold cross-border by investment firms under the MiFID passport in line with MiFID rules on suitability and appropriateness, but without any form of product regulation. This possible interpretation raises the broader question of product regulation *versus* services regulation in the sector, and the potential inconsistencies in the regulatory set-up. As for the indirect impact of MiFID on the sector, MiFID may well alter the execution landscape in the EEA (European Economic Area) and engender new forms of market structure, changes to which asset management firms will have to remain attuned.

This CEPS–ECMI Task Force met four times over the period of one year and reviewed the challenges facing the asset management industry, and particularly fund management. Based on input from business representatives, regulators and academics, the Task Force has formulated six broad recommendations aimed at policy-makers and an additional three addressed to the industry.

Recommendations to policy-makers:

1.   **The ongoing UCITS review is too limited in scope, and it should therefore be expanded beyond facilitating market integration to include a fundamental review of UCITS product regulation.** The ongoing review focuses almost exclusively on the functioning of the UCITS passport and the efficiency of the pan-European market for UCITS. While these efforts are welcomed, they do not address some more fundamental points on whether the UCITS regime is flexible enough to respond to the challenges it faces from alternative investment schemes and other products that are not regulated at European level and whether the restrictions on investment strategy and asset allocation that are embedded in it adequately reflect the lessons of modern portfolio theory. To this effect, the European Commission needs to shape a regulatory level playing field for economically similar products, stimulating a convergence of regulatory regimes across sectors (banking, insurance, asset management). It would also do well to reflect more widely on the existing framework on eligible assets and study the merits of moving UCITS towards a risk-based approach to investment strategies. If such an extension of eligible assets is not undertaken, the existing 'UCITS brand' will become old-fashioned very soon and will not be able to keep pace with innovation.

2.   The UCITS review needs to **make full use of the opportunities created by the 'Lamfalussy approach'.** Given the rapidly changing industry context, the updated UCITS Directive should be of the Lamfalussy type and allow for rapid changes to be introduced in line with market developments, as is the case with MiFID. Such a shift is especially important in the context of the debate on eligible assets, as the accelerating pace of innovation in the sector will make it increasingly difficult for the existing regulatory framework to keep pace.

3.   It is critical that the European Commission gives further **guidance on the interaction between UCITS and MiFID** to the industry, as confusion still reigns in the marketplace and among regulatory authorities. In the absence of clear guidance from the European

Commission and CESR (Committee of European Securities Regulators) on how these two directives fit together, an uneven playing field may emerge, not only in the distribution of UCITS post-MiFID, but also in the distribution of unregulated products. To the detriment of market efficiency, such a situation could encourage firms to engage in regulatory arbitrage through the creation and distribution of financial instruments that synthetically replicate UCITS risk-return profiles, but do not meet the investment constraints imposed by UCITS rules.

4. **Allowing a real Management Company passport** – which the UCITS Directive did not make clear enough – would go a long way towards removing the significant degree of legal doubt that prevails today and that handicaps the management company passport. The supervisory framework of management companies still has to be urgently improved and the respective responsibilities more clearly allotted between home and host country authorities.

5. **Putting in place an intermediate and flexible common framework for private placements** is essential. Across Europe today, there is a wide mix of private placement regimes, ranging from none at all, to very liberal to very strict. The confusing array of different regimes and the lack of consistency is striking, leading to various forms of arbitrage and an uneven playing field. Such a situation is very costly for the institutional market, with negative consequences for market efficiency and competitiveness. It also hampers the creation of a single European market for wealth management, as private banks rely extensively on private placement rules in selling alternative investments to their clients. Constraining the emergence of a pan-European market for wealth management will likely have adverse consequences on the industry and the wider European economy, and is inconsistent with an era where citizens and workers are increasingly mobile and where private wealth is proliferating at a rapid pace. The market cannot afford to wait several years for such a framework to be developed, and therefore legislative activity to this effect should be accelerated. But such a private placement regime will only facilitate the offer of funds, in particular alternative investments: it will not ease the allowance for institutional investors to invest in such funds, as long as the current definition of eligible assets under UCITS remains unchanged (see point 1).

6.   Given the chequered experience with implementing a convergent approach to the calculation of Total Expense Ratios (TERs) under the Commission's 2004 Recommendation, whereby divergent national interpretations have resulted in quasi-incomparable expense ratios, **the Commission and CESR should work on a common definition of TERs for UCITS.** Because of the increasing convergence between traditional long-only funds and alternative investments, **the Commission and CESR should also reflect on how consistent – yet flexible – TERs could be developed to span the entirety of the collective investments universe, including unregulated funds. The Commission should also remain vigilant with respect to the interpretation of MiFID Art. 19 (3) on transparency of costs and related fees, in particular with regard to UCITS.** If not, distributors of funds whose home member states have stricter fee disclosure rules (e.g. requiring the disclosure of hard-to-calculate transaction costs) will face a significant disadvantage *vis-à-vis* their competitors.

Recommendations to the industry:

1.   **Clarify the respective roles, responsibilities and liabilities of the fund manufacturer and distributor in a common way across the EU.** Such agreements are a vital element in ensuring the proper functioning of open architecture models of distribution. The nature and content of these agreements ought to be made under an industry code of conduct spearheaded by industry associations in consultation with regulators, rather than legislated.

2.   **Distributors adopting a guided architecture model ought to disclose in a transparent and visible way the criteria used in the selection of third-party and own funds placed on the shelf in a fund supermarket.** Initially, the format of the disclosure could be designed through an industry code of conduct, but if it is not effective, the Commission ought to take steps to enforce a common format. Despite their advantages, guided architecture models may be discriminated against by regulators in favour of open architecture models, precisely because the selection process for admitting third party products onto a distribution platform is seen by regulators and clients to be a black box – possibly giving the impression that the product selection process is biased towards those providers who pay higher distribution fees. If properly implemented, MiFID rules on conflict of interest and inducements should shed more light on the

product selection and distribution process, giving regulators and clients more confidence in its robustness.

3. **Adopt a European standard that establishes a uniform approach to the calculation and presentation of performance results**. In line with Recommendation 6 above, the industry should seize the initiative to develop a pan-European standard on performance attribution and reporting. A uniform standard will facilitate the comparison of financial results across the EU, leading to a more efficient investment market and to a higher degree of investor protection. A fragmented framework on performance reporting – as with TERs – prevents a truly competitive market from emerging, as the value-for-money investors get from different fund managers cannot be compared in a clear and consistent manner.

INTRODUCTION

The European fund management industry has undergone profound changes since the 1985 UCITS (Undertakings for Collective Investment in Transferable Securities) Directive. Today, there are about 32,000 UCITS products, representing over €6 trillion of assets under management.[1] These facts point to the success of the UCITS brand as one that is operational and reliable, all the while securing a high degree of investor protection.

Nevertheless, despite its successes, the UCITS framework has shown signs of weakness: the very concept of UCITS might have to be revised, as the brand struggles to keep pace with the evolution and the rapid rate of innovation in the marketplace. Today, about half of the new cash raised is not channelled into UCITS products, but rather into alternative funds – hedge funds/funds of hedge funds; real estate funds; private equity funds; and structured product wrappers around these funds – all of which are unregulated at EU level so far. At the same time, due to remaining regulatory barriers, full-scale cross-border consolidation in the sector and cross-border management of funds has not really taken off, pointing to the unsatisfactory result of economies of scale left unexploited: cross-border sales only account for 17% of UCITS funds under management, although the degree of penetration of foreign funds admittedly varies considerably from country to country. Despite the obvious successes of the UCITS regime, in particular the export of UCITS funds all over the world, the limited degree of cross-border consolidation within the EU has been frustrating to the European Commission in its 20-year old quest to deliver a truly single market for asset management in the EU, strengthening its

---

[1] See statistics in Annex 1 at the end of this report.

resolve to make the pan-European market more efficient. Indeed, the sector has been identified as one of the Commission's top priorities in the post-FSAP (Financial Services Action Plan) agenda, as confirmed by the publishing of a Green Paper on the enhancement of the EU framework for investment funds in July 2005 and a White Paper in November 2006.

At the heart of the current debate is whether, going forward, the UCITS framework can provide the sort of flexibility that is conducive to developing a competitive and efficient market for fund management across the EU without damaging UCITS' reputation as a hallmark of investor protection. The need for flexibility in UCITS entails two dimensions: one on the product level, the other on the institutional level.

On the product level, the emergence of new (and exotic) financial instruments and investment strategies has raised a debate on (re-)defining asset eligibility for UCITS, and the investment restrictions they face. The question is a delicate one, as it navigates a difficult trade-off between investor protection and efficiency/innovation. As industry structures evolve and new products appear, the trade-off will become more manifest, and conflicts of interest will become more prevalent. Policy discussions now revolve around whether and to what extent the MiFID framework for addressing conflicts of interest can be applied to UCITS, and how it would have to be modified to this end.

On the institutional level, the fact that the UCITS legislative process does not fully operate within the Lamfalussy framework means that there are still impediments to the quick and smooth adoption of legislation, which can evidently have repercussions on the performance of the industry. Significant amendments were applied to the original UCITS Directive in 2001 in an urgent need to update the original legislation. In particular, the new UCITS regime was based on a 'Product Directive', which expanded the range of financial instruments that could qualify as eligible investments under UCITS, and a 'Management Company Directive', which set harmonised operational criteria for management companies and introduced the simplified prospectus. Despite these improvements, and the targeted Level 2 measure adopted by the Commission in 2007 regarding eligible assets, it remains debatable whether the EU's current legislative framework covering the asset management industry accurately reflects the structural changes that have been precipitated by the rapid pace of innovation and the emergence of new financial instruments, continuing disintermediation and the first moves towards a pan-European open architecture in fund distribution.

Finally, there are critically important competition issues in the European fund industry that arise around charging structures. Introducing greater transparency in the breakdown of costs, including trading commissions, distribution fees, subscription and redemption fees, performance fees and other charges, is one way to enhance competition. This is all the more necessary, given that in a number of continental countries, the distribution of third-party products is often hampered by high distribution charges imposed by local banks, which enjoy a virtual monopoly in the distribution of financial products to the retail market, and render the penetration of potentially better-performing competing funds more difficult.

This report is structured as follows. Chapters 1 and 2 sketch the size of the fund management industry and its organisational structure in the EU and the different EU member states. They set the framework for the discussions in chapters 3 and 4 on the regulatory framework for fund management in the EU and the interaction with the MiFID.

1. THE EUROPEAN ASSET MANAGEMENT INDUSTRY: A SURVEY

The European asset management industry plays a crucial role in Europe's economy. It comprises all actors (insurance companies, banks, investment funds, pension funds, etc.) that operate in financial markets, investing savings of retail and institutional investors in capital and money markets. The huge diversity in the European asset management business both in terms of products and services makes it impossible to give a precise estimate of the industry that manages over ten trillion euros in assets.[2]

The differences in regulatory frameworks across Europe make the picture even more complex, but they are key to grasping a better understanding of the different investment choices in each member state. These differences are mainly linked to different behaviour on the part of investors and to the evolution of financial markets across Europe. For example, investors in English-speaking countries invest more in equity markets entrusting their capital to stockbrokers rather than to banks, while in the rest of Europe, banks have been and remain the dominant distributors of funds.[3]

In recent years an overall change in this trend has been observed. The Directive governing Undertakings for Collective Investment in

---

[2] This value stems from the sum of the assets of investment funds, life insurance and occupational pension funds.

[3] A Feri Fund Market Information survey conducted on the distribution channels in France, Germany, Italy, Spain and UK shows that the banking sector in the UK accounts only for 14% of assets under management (AuM) against an average of 61% in other European countries.

Transferable Securities (UCITS), Solvency II and the Markets in Financial Instruments Directive (MiFID) represent a normative answer to this evolving situation that has been carrying the industry market forward to a more complex financial situation. Another important necessary change for many states was that of reforming pension systems by means of the introduction of funded elements to complement the pay-as-you-go (PAYG) structure. As a consequence of such reform, insurance companies have started to get involved in pension investments. Insurance companies have recently achieved high levels of asset growth: 6.2% in 2003 and 9.3% in 2004. In 2005, insurers managed approximately 20% of the total pensions contributions, accumulating an amount of reserves of more than €2,200 billion. In volume terms, however, after decades of dominance of the insurance sector, investment fund assets started from 2005 onwards to represent the single most important category, accounting for 55.1% of GDP against 51.8% of insurance funds and 22.2% of pension funds (see Annex 1). In relative terms, however, cross-country differences still persist. The statistics show that Luxembourg and France lead the investment funds scene with a market share of almost 45% in 2007. In 2006, the UK, Germany and France represented 65% of the life and non-life businesses and in 2005, the total assets managed by pension funds in the Netherlands were at least double that of every other European country (on a pro rata basis).

1.1 Investment funds

Since 2002, total assets under management (AuM) in European investment funds have achieved a remarkable development, growing 24% over the last four years as a percentage of GDP. In particular, between 2004 and 2006, the total assets managed by UCITS and non-UCITS funds have been undergoing a comparable growth: the former by 54% and the latter by 52%.[4] In terms of assets in the last five years, the relationship between UCITS and non-UCITS products has not changed: in July 2007, UCITS products accounted for 79% of AuM against 21% of non-UCITS products

---

[4] The main distinction between UCITS and non-UCITS instruments is in the asset allocation and the geographical scope (European for UCITS, national for the others) and the difference in levels of control. As UCITS are usually sold to retail investors, they need to be subject to stricter rules than non–UCITS, which are generally sold to institutional investors.

(these percentage shares have remained stable since 1993).[5] As of 2002, the non-UCITS industry has been boosted by the development of hedge funds reaching an impressive level of growth (more than 100% between 2002 and 2006). However, the bigger category in terms of size has been that of special funds reserved for institutional investors. These special funds recorded a 47% asset growth during the period 2004-06 and in 2006 held 58% of non-UCITS assets.

Based on the experience of more than 20 years after the entry into force of the UCITS Directive, first adopted in 1985, the UCITS model has proved itself to be a success. Today there are over 32,000 UCITS funds, spread across Europe, Asia and Latin America,[6] with about six trillion assets under management. Europe comes second, right behind the US, as the largest fund manager in the world (33% of the world market share against 50% for the US). Between 2004 and July 2007, the European investment fund industry achieved an estimated €2,726 billion growth of AuM, 56% of which is accounted for by net sales, with the remaining part attributable to market appreciation.

Among the different UCITS instruments, equity funds are by far the most important category of UCITS investment type. Between 2004 and July 2007, market participants increased their investments in this sector by 78%, moving its absolute portfolio weight, among all categories of investment funds, up from 35% to 41%. These good performances, linked to the bull market that started after the end of TMT (technology, media and telecoms) bubble (end 2002), could be explained both by growing investments in funds and by a higher performance in terms of risk-return of equity investments – a key factor in the appreciation of equity indices. In particular in 2006, Luxembourg ranked first with €84 billion in net sales, immediately followed by France (€48 billion) and the UK (€10 billion).

The second category in terms of AuM is bonds. In 2006 the high level of inflow in Luxembourg (€40 billion) compensated the outflow experienced by many European countries, especially Italy (-€36 billion),

---

[5] See European Commission (2006b, p. 10).

[6] UCITS is well appreciated in non-EU countries because of the strict regulatory regime. UCITS are thus perceived as one of the best regulated investment product, also because, since their introduction, they have never triggered any financial scandals.

amounting to a positive total net flow of €5 billion (+4% compared to 2005). In any event, since 2002 the bond market has lost part of its attractiveness because of the decline in interest rates. Between 2002 and 2006, based upon a hypothetical portfolio composed of all types of UCITS investment products, the weighted share of bonds has fallen by 7.6%.

Money markets experienced a similar decline for the same reasons. Data show that between 2002 and 2006 the weight of this segment fell by 4.3% with respect to the absolute UCITS portfolio value, although AuM managed by money funds stayed at the same level in 2006 as in 2005. One would, however, have expected a more pronounced decline given the very low levels of short-term interest rates in that period. In France, for example, the money market sector is still extremely important, generating inflows of €29.8 billion in 2006, €29.7 billion in 2005 and €16.7 billion in 2004.

A closer look at the data reveals that since 2002 equity funds have performed very well. In the last four years these funds have grown by €345 billion, marking a sharp increase (25%) between 2005 and 2006. The development of these funds is both linked to the strong performance of equity markets as such and to sophisticated investors' demand for more specialised types of financial instruments.[7]

Overall, the geographical distribution of investment funds is heterogeneous (see Figure 1). In June 2007, Luxembourg and France together counted for more than 50% of the total UCITS markets. This high market share is explained by the attractive regulatory framework in Luxembourg and the strong demand for money market funds in France (representing 52% of the European market).[8]

One measure of the heterogeneity of the European market is the difference in the fund sizes in different countries. By the end of June 2007, the average size per fund in Europe was €189 million. Considering only the countries with more than €100 million of AuM per fund, the most concentrated markets were Italy (€329 million), the UK (€317 million) and Sweden (€285 million). At the opposite extreme there were Belgium, Austria and Spain with €72 million, €81 million and €100 million, respectively.

---

[7] See below, chapter 2.

[8] For more details, see Table A2, Statistics on Asset Management, Annex 1.

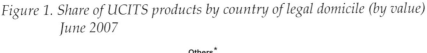

Figure 1. Share of UCITS products by country of legal domicile (by value)
June 2007

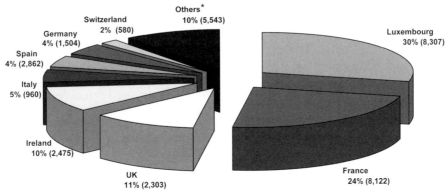

Note: The numbers in parentheses indicate the number of funds per country.

* Others include Austria, Belgium, Finland, Greece, the Netherlands, Portugal, Denmark and Sweden.

Source: EFAMA.

In terms of preferred instruments, equity funds are the most important category of funds in Sweden, the UK, the Netherlands and Norway, whereas bond funds are very popular in Denmark, Portugal, Spain and Austria. The asset management industry in Turkey, Slovakia and the Czech Republic is driven by money funds. These differences in investment decisions reflect, on the one hand, different commercial strategies and investment objectives of institutional investors and individual citizens (demand side) and, on the other hand, the fragmentation of the investment fund structure (supply side), as underlined in the distribution and manufacturing elements of the value chain.[9] Moreover, differences in investment behaviour between countries reduce the level of competition among European investment funds and thus also the degree of market integration.

The European market is not a uniform, homogeneous platform. Similar funds of small size, for instance, are developed in different member

---

[9] In 2005, banks were the most dominant fund distributors in Europe, accounting for 52% of the total net assets (TNA); the unique exception was the UK with 47% of TNA managed by independent advisers (see next chapter).

states. Investors prefer to operate on a domestic basis and successful distributors of products are not marketing all funds across Europe. Data show that in 2004 only 17% of the funds on the European market were sold on a cross-border basis and that almost 63% of cross-border sales originated from Luxembourg and 12% from Dublin.[10] These two places are clearly attractive because of the lenient tax regimes and lower trade restrictions. In particular, one may find complex funds for institutional investors in Dublin, whereas Luxembourg tends to be a domicile for 'easy', non-complex products. The growth of cross-border activity has important repercussions for the European market in terms of opportunities, efficiency and scale benefits.

A comparison between the European market (young and fragmented) and the US market (well developed and homogenous) could help to understand the quantitative gap to be overcome (see Figure 2):

- The number of European funds is four times higher than in the US.

- Total European assets account for three-quarters of mutual fund assets in the US.

- But the average size of an investment fund in Europe is less than one-fifth that of American funds.

Figure 2. Comparison of average investment fund size in Europe and the US, end 2006

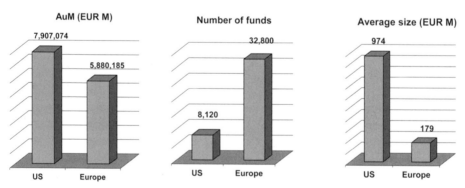

Note: Numbers may not fully correspond with EFAMA data.
Source: ICI.

---

[10] PwC (2006), "Pan European UCITS Distribution 2005".

The sub-optimal average UCITS size may bring about higher operational costs for investment management, a high total expense ratio (TER)[11] and duplication of infrastructure. In this sense, the asset management industry performs below its possibilities, the cost of which is passed on to the user. The main causes are to be found in the high level of fragmentation, the absence among investors and firms of a European market concept and the remunerative *niche* markets that funds can target, exploiting differences in tax and regulatory regimes across Europe.

It should be emphasised that fragmentation is the most crucial issue in Europe: it reduces competition,[12] affects supply and demand, limits the potential synergies and cost savings in organisational, distribution and manufacturing activities among similar financial organisations, and reduces the choice for users. Moreover, low levels of homogeneity, which increases the national orientation of firms and investors, weaken the capacity of the industry to achieve economies of scale.

Investors also encounter other problems: i) high costs of entry, ii) the general perception of the low level of competition and iii) lack of clear information regarding costs and risks of particular investment funds. On the other hand, industry's inefficiency is mainly caused by: i) long delays and high costs in authorisation and notification procedures and ii) the lack of standardised processing systems.[13] These issues are at the centre of the current investigations by the European Commission.

The relatively small average size of investment funds is also linked to another trend in the asset management industry: the proliferation of new funds responding to evolving investors' needs (fund of hedge funds, fund

---

[11] For a definition of TER, see chapter 2.

[12] A measure of competition for cross-country comparisons is the level of market concentration for the top five asset managers (AMs). The most competitive countries are the UK and Ireland with 28% of the total net assets allocated to the top five AMs, followed by France (41%) and Germany (46%), while the East European countries are the most concentrated (see ZEW, 2006, p. 5).

[13] European Commission (2006a), White Paper on Enhancing the Single Market Framework for Investment Funds.

of funds of hedge funds, private equity funds, real estate funds[14]) and to new business opportunities (green funds, ethical funds, infrastructure funds) that reach high levels of income.[15] In the first seven months of 2007, €4.6 billion of net inflows into equity funds across Europe went into green funds.[16] In particular, the phenomenal growth of the hedge funds industry (Figure 3), with more than €1 trillion under management, places this financial product as a dominant force in the global fund management industry. Today hedge funds have achieved an overall acceptance both among distributors and investors. From the distribution side, for instance, banks deal with hedge funds in order to get involved in a lucrative business while diversifying income sources. Moreover, in relation to the development of hedge funds, new third party distributors, especially funds of funds (FoF) and managers of managers (MoM) are growing rapidly.

Funds of hedge funds allow for a better diversification. They exploit the knowledge of different groups of specialists and, in so doing, have a deep impact on hedge funds themselves. An analysis conducted by the *Hedge Funds Research* on its databases suggested that recently, funds of funds have rapidly grown. Data, published by *Pensions & Investment,* showed that in 2006 funds of hedge funds accounted for 44% of the total value of the hedge fund industry, compared to 36% in 2005 and 17% in 2000.[17] A study conducted by Greenwich Associates (2006) shows the importance of hedge funds in terms of global liquidity of financial markets. One of the main findings is that the hedge fund industry is deeply involved in the markets, with different percentages in the overall trading volume: 47% in emerging market bonds, 55% in credit derivatives market and an important chunk of equity trading volume.

---

[14] While in 2002 only 7% of AuM invested in non-UCITS market was explained by hedge funds investments, in 2006 the market share claimed by hedge funds has reached 15% (authors' own estimate based on ECB and EFAMA reports).

[15] A survey conducted by La Caixa has compared the annualised return of NASDAQ, Eurostoxx 50 and the hedge funds present in the Tremont database. The study found that during the period 1994-2006, hedge funds' annualised returns were the highest, reaching 11% of their initial investments. NASDAQ came in second with 9.5%, and Eurostoxx 50 third (9.2%) (see La Caixa, 2007).

[16] *Financial Times*, 24 September 2007.

[17] *Pensions & Investments*, 17 September 2007.

As for the regulatory responses, authorities in the US and Europe are coming to grips with how to respond to the growth of hedge funds. The US Securities and Exchange Commission (SEC) on the one side and the European regulators on the other are considering the setting of new rules in order to better regulate the instrument without undermining its extraordinary evolution. Notably, there is an ongoing debate in Europe about the possibility to include alternative investments in the UCITS regime.

Figure 3. The European hedge fund industry

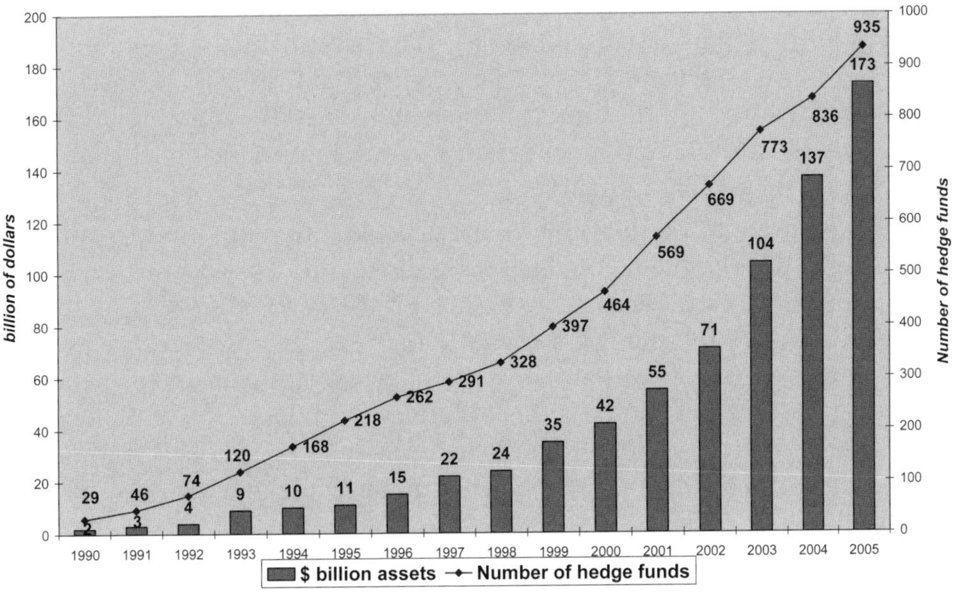

Source: ECB; authors' own estimates for number of hedge funds in 2005.

1.2 Insurance companies

Some 82% of the insurance industry is composed of life business, with the remaining part being non-life. In the last four years, this sector has seen constant growth, with total assets in the EU 25 of €6,510 billion in 2006 (representing an increase of 5.3% as compared to 2005) and a premium income of €1,065 billion. This premium income is composed of €659 billion in the life business (6.5% more than 2005) and of €406 billion in non-life business (an increase of 5.3% with respect to 2005).[18] A closer look at life business reveals two different aspects. First, unit-linked products have become more and more attractive in some markets; it can be assumed that their success was supported by good performance in the stock market. Secondly, insurers manage approximately 20% of the occupational pension contributions market.

A different situation characterises the non-life products. In fact, apart from the exceptional event of privatisation of the Dutch health insurance system, an overall slowdown in the market can be observed. In 2006, excluding the Dutch privatisation, the annual growth rate would have been 1%, and 0.6% in 2005, reflecting high levels of competition in this sector. This is further emphasised by the fact that investments in insurance assets represent 54.6% of the GDP in 2006 against 51.8% in 2005. Consequently, there is a positive trend, starting immediately after the bursting of the dot-com bubble in 2001, which mirrors the rising importance of this sector in the asset management industry.

It is important to highlight a remarkable difference among countries. The high development of life insurance and, in several cases, the development of new pension insurance products stand at 80% to 100% of GDP in Switzerland, the UK, Denmark and Sweden. At the other extreme, East European countries have low levels of investments, even if they are growing faster than some other Western countries. Luxembourg and Liechtenstein are considered outliers with insurance assets standing at more than three times GDP, which can be explained by low levels of taxation.

In terms of asset allocation, insurance funds have invested mainly in domestic fixed income, with the historical exception of the UK, Ireland and Sweden. These three countries have invested an average of 53% in equity and about 36% in domestic fixed income. Nevertheless, in recent decades, the difference between English-speaking countries and the rest of Europe has become less pronounced. In the UK, investment in domestic fixed income increased a total of 12% in the last six years – a clear signal of the convergence process in European markets.

---

[18] This high level of growth rate in non-life business is mostly explained by the privatisation of the health insurance system in the Netherlands.

As with the European investment fund market, the European insurance market is characterised by a generalised lack of harmonisation among different states. There are several differences in the way in which supervision is conducted and each country has set out its own minimum solvency margin requirement. Other differences regard the procedure applied to investment assessment and technical provisions.[19] In addition, the gap across European countries has further increased with the development of new insurance products in financial markets, actuarial sciences and risk management. It is undeniable that public intervention in an important sector like insurance is necessary. However, differences in regulatory frameworks across Europe reduce the international competitiveness of insurance companies and increase the possibility of regulatory arbitrage.

1.3 Pension funds

The pension fund industry has resumed a positive trend after the drop of the early years of this century, coinciding with the equity markets downturn in 2000-03. At the end of 2005, EU pension funds managed €2,583 billion, achieving a growth rate of 19% in the last 3 years.[20]

Investment behaviour is more similar across countries than across sectors: Northern Europe invests mainly in equity, while the rest of the continent prefers fixed income. In particular, the Netherlands, Finland and the UK register an increment in equity investment connected to the reallocation of their portfolio linked to the slump in equity markets. On the other hand, bonds play the dominant role in France, Denmark and Spain.

---

[19] A problem that European authorities have to face is the lack of risk sensitivity in the calculation of the solvency margin. This formula in fact does not include market, credit and operational risk and mitigation tools, such as reinsurance, securitisations or derivatives, are not used. The main consequences are that insurance companies cannot manage their risks appropriately and have a sub-optimal allocation of capital, while supervisors have very little room for intervention.

[20] The most developed is the Netherlands with a pension fund market of 124.9% of GDP, while at the bottom is Belgium, with 4.2% of GDP. However, in the latter case, most pension funds are organised group insurance schemes, and are reported statistically under that sector.

This difference in asset allocation could be explained by persistent differences in pension schemes. A distinction needs to be made between the so-called 'first pillar' and the 'second pillar'. The first is public and financed by social security and tax revenues, while the second pillar is characterised by professional contributions that are privately managed and invested. By September 2005, all EU states implemented Directive (2003/41) on Institutions for Occupational Retirement Provision (IORP) into their national legislation, which abolishes quantitative investment restrictions for investments of 'second pillar' pension plans and replaces these by a series of qualitative criteria. Countries that maintain quantitative criteria can only do this within their national boundaries.

The first pillar of the pension systems is quite varied among the EU member states, and some countries, in order to reduce pension expenditure and to support the traditional PAYG schemes, have set up reserve funds and/or statutory-funded pension schemes.[21] Different sets of legislation have established rules for reserve funds and statutory-funded pension schemes. In order to guarantee a risk profile reflecting investors' needs, the legislators set forth quantitative and qualitative portfolio restrictions. The most common restrictions are: transaction cost, internal investment guidelines, exchange rate risk, asymmetric information, tax, political risk and purchasing power risk. These restrictions tend to reduce and sometimes impede foreign investment.

In Belgium, for example, special reserve funds can only invest in domestic bonds.[22] A similar obligation is in place in Portugal, requiring 50% investment in government debt and limiting the remaining part of the investment to a maximum exposure of 15% for unhedged currencies. Funded first-pillar pension schemes in Bulgaria, Hungary and Poland are obliged by legislation to invest 90% of their assets domestically. There are also exceptions, however. No limits have been imposed by Ireland and

---

[21] Currently 9 out of 27 countries have introduced these statutory funds and pension schemes, namely Bulgaria, Denmark, Estonia, Hungary, Latvia, Lithuania, Poland, Slovakia and Sweden.

[22] Reserve funds can be found in Belgium, Cyprus, Finland, France, Ireland, Luxembourg, the Netherlands, Poland, Portugal, Spain and Sweden (see Oxera, 2007).

Luxembourg in the demographic reserve funds, nor by Sweden and Latvia for the funded first-pillar pension plans.

An Oxera (2007) study has analysed the potential benefit of international diversification for such funds using the mean-variance approach, comparing the domestic equity market returns of France, Germany, Italy, the Netherlands, Sweden and the UK with a portfolio investing 60% domestically and 40% in a European index and with 100% diversified European portfolio. All countries experienced an improvement in the descriptive parameters, especially in terms of portfolio volatility. Although one can observe a lower level of average returns in Sweden (0.156%) and the UK (-0.349%), they are counterbalanced by a higher decline of volatility levels, 1.082% and 1.863%, respectively.[23] This means that a greater diversification across European equity generates a lower level of risk. But unfortunately investment restrictions limits the ability of an asset manager to achieve better performances. International investment in bond markets shows different results with lower portfolio performance.

1.4 Concluding remarks

As stated from the outset, it is very difficult to predict the evolution of the European asset management industry. Investment, insurance and pension funds sectors are changing very quickly and the debate about how to regulate the sector has to take European market developments into account.

Internal and external factors may reduce the attractiveness of European asset management, and in particular the UCITS brand. On the one hand, the low level of cross-border operations are symptomatic of the fragmentation of the European market (which lowers returns and reduces competition, hence allowing the development of niche markets that otherwise would not exist). On the other hand, the growing proliferation since 2002 of sophisticated non-UCITS products, regulated by national legislators, is reducing the level of harmonisation in European fund management markets introduced by the UCITS regime. This underlines the

---

[23] The average return and the level of variance are considered valid estimations, respectively, of expected return and associated risk of the financial operation. A reduction of the returns' mean could be well balanced by a lower level of volatility.

necessity to define international rules for these new instruments that nowadays have achieved the same popularity among institutional and retail investors as UCITS products, such as hedge funds.[24]

The industry has reached a crossroads. The nature of risk is changing: a crisis in one sector or country has a contagious impact on other activities and countries, with amazing repercussions on the entire financial sector and hence economic growth. It is thus crucial to further integrate European markets, in order to improve the competitiveness of UCITS products and to update the procedures to simplify cross-border operations. Fund managers themselves should support European market integration to save costs and to have a larger demand to satisfy. The costs of current market fragmentation have been estimated by the INVESCO's Research Group at €6 billion for regulatory inefficiencies and between €2 to €6 billion per year for the lack of economies of scale.[25] These data are self-evident and their significant reduction deserves the highest attention in the name of market efficiency.

Box 1. Questions on the future of hedge funds to be borne in mind by regulators

Is it really worth regulating the hedge funds industry? Will it be beneficial for financial markets?

To answer this question, one cannot ignore the reasons why this instrument became so popular among investors. The introduction of hedge funds was not due to firms' strategies to reach more investors. On the contrary, the root of the emergence of hedge funds is to be found in investors' demands for innovation and more tailored services. Today, investors need flexible products that are able to keep up with market changes.

However, there is a recent trend towards a progressive (direct or indirect) 'retailisation' of this market.

---

[24] Whether a uniform code of law can be defined for the hedge funds industry is an open question. On one hand, it is necessary that the level of harmonisation of European markets is not threatened by the development of these products, but on the other hand, it is important to preserve the role they have achieved for investors (see Box 1).

[25] See INVESCO (2005).

What could be the effect of future legislative intervention aimed at regulating the product so as to set up a common product (in addition to keeping the existing national ones) in Europe?

It would depend how EU legislation would be oriented. If it were oriented towards a strict product regulation, the most likely effect on the product might be that of reducing the degree of freedom and making the product more standardised. Hedge funds would lose their originality and the segment of investors interested in investing in these products would change.

If the orientation of the relevant EU legislation were to set up a mixed product/player regulation, mainly focused on regulating the different players involved in the value chain (management companies, prime brokers/depositaries, etc.), then it would allow for a safe framework regarding the skills, organisation and functioning of these players while still keeping a high degree of flexibility for the product itself. Such a mixed product/players' regulation has already been tested successfully in several member states, and is probably the most appropriate way to set up an EU framework without harming the flexibility that is needed for such a product.

On an overall level, the current activism of the demand side could suggest that investors ask for new, innovative products. This could be an incentive for firms to enter into non-regulated businesses and could cause new problems for coordination in Europe. But developing a regulatory approach that focused more on regulation of the players than on product regulation could solve this issue, in particular if management companies are required to comply with a so-called 'activity programme' that shows their special skills, organisation and functioning for managing such funds. Clients would then have the possibility to choose between 'lightly' regulated hedge funds and unharmonised hedge funds.

This brings us back to the initial question: Would it be truly beneficial to regulate hedge fund markets?

In fact, if the scenario predicted above on the development of financial markets materialises, two general questions should be taken into account:

i) What is the cause of the emergence of a new financial product?

ii) What is the appropriate level of regulation for that instrument?

With this in mind, the European Commission's work to regulate hedge funds will be not an easy task, because, on one side, it is necessary to define a common platform across Europe, but on the other side the new rules should not change the intrinsic nature of the financial product. That is why developing product regulation should mainly focus on regulating the relevant players (for more, see EFAMA & Assogestioni, 2005).

2. THE STRUCTURE OF THE INVESTMENT FUNDS INDUSTRY

While in the past investment funds activities in Europe took place within the organisational structure of a bank, today funds have achieved high levels of autonomy. Banks have outsourced elements of the value chain (especially distribution and manufacturing), IT processing and entire business areas, and today the relationship between banks on the one side and UCITS and alternative funds on the other is not so clear.

In the course of the past five years, the structure of the investment funds industry has been strongly influenced by the emergence of a variety of financial developments and by the resulting need to amend and update the regulatory framework. With regard to the multifaceted range of financial developments, it is worth mentioning, inter alia, the significant evolution of the demand side, the new challenges brought about by the globalisation process and unprecedented innovation in information technology.

Within this framework, the role of investors in asset management decisions has changed. While in the 1990s, banks offered financial products and services to passive customers, today's investors are active takers. They are constantly assessing the information available on the market, continuously monitoring management actions and demanding better-performing instruments. Nowadays, investors take an active role, not only seeking high levels of return in the short run, but also requiring firms to adapt their business models to customer needs, in order to provide them with a truly tailored service. Institutional investors, retail investors and large shareholders have become one of the most important drivers in the decision-making process of fund strategies.

The most significant development for banks is the possibility to run their business in a more flexible way, related to different factors: i) the possibilities offered by globalisation to create and supply sophisticated financial products simultaneously in different markets; ii) the high level of obsolescence of IT programmes used to price complex financial instruments and iii) the general downturn of financial markets after the turn of the millennium, which became particularly evident at the bursting of the dotcom bubble and 9/11.

As for the responses provided by European regulators, one cannot disregard the huge impact from the introduction, in 2002, of the UCITS Management Company Directive (better known as UCITS III), which introduced a new 'Management Company Passport' allowing in principle a management company to carry out cross-border investment services, in particular direct cross-border management of funds. Moreover, by allowing funds to broaden the supply of financial instruments (like derivatives products), UCITS III has significantly boosted the shift in structuring European funds to an indefinite number of potential entities. This reform was supposed to facilitate European financial integration by virtue of the reduced cross-border barriers for services and marketing activities.

The cumulative effect of all these regulatory factors has pushed the market towards higher standards of sophistication and complexity. Speed to market and innovation became, day by day, fundamental elements of competitiveness for all financial intermediaries. The key challenge for financial actors now is to focus on more strategic issues like outsourcing non-core business areas that can be handled by third parties. Hence, the prevalent concept to be translated into practice is the preference of variable costs over fixed costs[26] and a stronger focus on core investment business, for firms to be able to respond to customers' needs in real time.

The changes in the structure of the investment fund industry have affected manufacturing and distribution channels of the value chain. This consideration becomes clear in light of three issues: i) the development of

---

[26] The reduction of fixed costs contributes to the creation of a more flexible structure, ready to be modified in response to market changes. From an economic point, the reduction of fixed costs aims to reduce a firm's unit costs to achieve the breakeven point (level of revenue necessary to cover fixed cost and hence to maintain the activity) faster. Moreover, it helps increase financial flexibility.

distribution channels in the last five years; ii) the processes of outsourcing by small- and medium-sized firms and iii) M&As of bigger firms.

With regard to the increased level of independence between funds and banks, a survey conducted by ZEW/OEE (2006) focusing on distribution channels in European countries, shows that in Europe in the period 2000-05, the percentage of fund assets managed by banks decreased by 7%. In France and the UK,[27] retail and private banks accounted in 2005 for less than 50% of assets under management. Moreover in France, Germany, Italy, Spain, Switzerland and UK, the market share of traditional distributors (insurance companies and banks) fell by 22% between 1990 and 2005. These statistics are evidence of a gradual opening up of the traditional distribution model and of the emergence of a guided architecture in the distribution market. Changing demand on the part of investors and their needs for greater transparency (especially in complex products) have been pushing managers to investigate and to develop new distribution channels, resulting in a generalised broadening of the traditional distribution channels to non-proprietary funds. Nowadays, independent financial advisors (IFAs – distributors not linked to an asset management firm of a financial group), NINFAs (distributors associated with a financial group that develops in-house products), Fund of Funds and Manager of Managers (distributors that offer articulated combinations of financial products and services) are the main third-party distributors available to asset management firms.

The manufacturing industry has also experienced a transformation of its structure in line with the fund dimensions and its capacity to generate new financial resources. Small- and medium-sized firms have represented the main examples of this trend of outsourcing. They function like 'independent boutiques' specialised in advanced financial instruments. This new vertical fragmentation is meant to exploit potential in-house strengths and to allow the outsourcing of activities in which the firm lacks adequate knowledge or IT platforms. In the case of vertical segmentation, funds generally prefer to deal with other specialised investment funds (hedge funds, funds of hedge funds or other alternative investment funds), rather than developing several in-house innovative businesses. This

---

[27] In the UK, in particular, the biggest slice belongs to independent financial advisers (IFAs) with 47% of assets under management.

approach allows funds to get involved in a lucrative business and to achieve high levels of diversification and liquidity offering their customers more tailored products, while exploiting bigger platforms of trade possibilities, dealing with different partners and intermediaries. Data confirm this trend: in 2006, the market for outsourcing in the banking sector totalled €9.8 billion, a growth of 9% as compared to 2005 (see Figure 4).

The ZEW/OEE (2006) report indicates how well the practice of outsourcing has developed in the UK and Ireland, while being least developed in Spain and Belgium. In Europe, the main administration functions outsourced in 2005 were third-party custody, fund administration and transfer agents, representing, respectively, 39%, 23% and 25% of total assets (see Oxera, 2006, p. 125).

Figure 4. Outsourcing levels in the European fund management sector (€ billion)

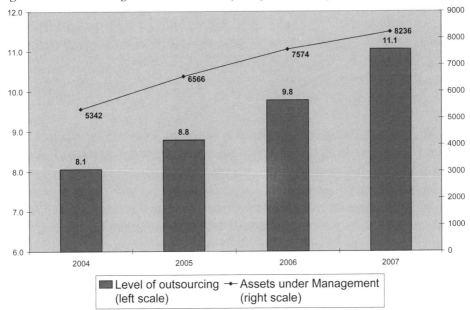

Source: PAC, EFAMA.

Coupled with the vertical integration described above, especially in the case of large financial institutions, high levels of competition and increased power of investors have fostered horizontal consolidation. These firms, in response to a core satellite approach of small funds and to the growing sophistication of financial products as allowed by UCITS,[28] have been pursuing M&A activities in order to develop high skills in alternative asset classes and to be able to manage the risk inherent in take-overs.

Table 1. Number of fund mergers* (as a percentage of total number of funds)

	2002	2003	2004		2005	
Austria	1.5%	4.7%	3.8%	(1,993, 12.9%)	5.7%	(2,088, 25.1%)
Belgium	2.4%	7.8%	0.8%	(1,383, 10.3%)	2.8%	(1,501, -)
France	2.5%	2.1%	1.7%	(11,608, 10.1%)	3.5%	(11,536)
Germany	1.2%	0.8%	0.7%	(6,070, 3.2%)	1.4%	(5,971, 12.9%)
Italy	3.9%	15.1%	13.0%	(1,300, -1.8%)	12.2%	(1,237, 3.3%)
Spain	4.7%	7.5%	5.8%	(2,566, 14.5%)	6.4%	(2,679, 15.8%)
UK	1.6%	6.1%	3.4%	(2,280, 13%)	3.3%	(2,217, 28.8%)
EU	1.7%	2.8%	2.3%	(43,212, 10.9%)	2.7%	(44,342, 22.8)

* The number of funds and the growth rate in term of AuM are given between parentheses. No data are available for 2002 and 2003.
Source: ZEW/OEE (2006) and EFAMA.

An Oxera (2006) survey shows how the core asset management functions are concentrated in large financial centres, notably London, Paris and Frankfurt. The goal of these companies is to obtain benefits from merging similar funds into single common funds and to have a broad access to the European market. In particular, large investment companies, providing advanced financial services to money managers, hedge funds, market-makers, arbitrageurs, specialists and other professional investors, have become the most important prime brokers and the most professional third-parties entities, also in countries like Germany, France and Italy. Moreover, from 2002 to 2005, the numbers of national fund mergers

---

[28] Boosted by the evolution of hedge funds and the favourable rules, UCITS have been incorporating alternative and structured product. This new trend is called the 'commoditisation' of hedge funds.

increased in almost all European countries, except Portugal. Such growth has been particularly evident in Italy, Spain and Austria (see Table 1).[29]

The change in distribution structure and the vertical fragmentation along with the horizontal consolidation of investment funds have changed the relationship between manufacturing and distribution channels. The clearest evidence is the loss of market power for the manufacturing sector. The evolution of investor expectations, demanding more sophisticated products, coupled with the rise of third-party distributors,[30] have changed the rules of the market, shifting the bargaining power from the manufacturing to the distribution channels. As a result, we have witnessed the development of the so-called 'guided architecture' (as opposed to the 'open architecture').[31] In the guided architecture context, the choice of the right distribution partner becomes strategic for firms. Third-party distributors have to own qualitative and quantitative references. In particular, qualitative criteria refer typically to financial strength, financial stability, brand and penetration of the market (i.e. the range of general and specialised products offered). Quantitative criteria, on the other hand, refer mainly to the risk/return relationship of all funds involved in the sales process, the 'replicability' of the products (in term of difficulty for the competitors to replicate the portfolio assets) and relative performance of the selected fund against the benchmark. The main problem is to find distributors that possess all the above-mentioned characteristics. In case, however, third-parties distributors are able to live up to high quantitative and qualitative references, they may impose tight financial conditions. This is why the fund managers charge high fees to end-investors, as a result of the retrocession fees (i.e. the percentage of the so-called 'management fees' charged to investors) they have to pay to the best distributors.

---

[29] No data are available for cross-border mergers of funds, because of differences in national regulatory frameworks and tax regimes.

[30] Third-party distributors, exploiting the separation between the two channels of the value chain, have created a market niche, accounting for 25% of distribution market share in 2005.

[31] Under open architecture, banks allow the distribution of all funds available on the market, whereas under guided architecture, banks open their distribution networks to third-party funds, thereby allowing the distribution of a set of funds from pre-selected fund promoters.

2.1 Fee structure in the fund industry

The guided architecture has fostered competition among asset managers but, at the same time, has brought about new risks. From the investor's point of view, the ability of distributors to impose products on investors in the markets and the persisting asymmetric information between distributors (well informed) and investors (unable to fully evaluate the trade-off between risk and profit of sophisticated products) are the main causes of the new difficulties. Advanced products have been developed to better fit investors' demand, but the high levels of sophistication of these products create a huge gap between suppliers and end-investors. The asymmetric information could increase the incentive for distributors to pursue their own objectives more than the needs of the investor. Distributors, in fact, in accordance with the guided architecture, do not provide the full range of market products. Rather their supply is determined by their connections to a particular fund provider (tied distributors). As a result, they tend to recommend a particular fund or product in relation to the level of commission they will receive, reducing market efficiency and transparency.

The special relationship between investment fund managers and their distributors has the effect of increasing the costs borne by investors in terms of higher charges due to retrocession fees. Moreover, as a consequence of the open architecture and the increased bargaining power of distributors,[32] the typologies of deals between manufacturers and distributors have proliferated and become more and more articulated.[33]

---

[32] The retrocession fee is the best way to measure the growing bargaining power of distributors, as it shows the costs an asset manager has to have access to distribution. Retrocession fees are defined in relation to the assets under management (AuM) of a firm. Using this parameter it can be observed that in Germany, the UK and Spain, retrocession fees are lower in money market funds than in hedge funds and that in Italy and Spain, retrocession fees are highest. In these two countries, in fact, distributors used to get a commission respectively equal to 1.10% and 0.98% of AuM.

[33] Distributors could agree with manufacturers (asset managers) to offer to the end investors only the products made in-house. Alternatively, they could complete the range of products offered including external products from competitors; or, in extreme cases, they could decide to replace the products offered by in-house

Hence, alternative fee structures have started to multiply. These fees structures are mostly opaque, as fund managers do not specify how fees are broken down in the value chain.[34]

In 2005 retrocession fees were most important for equity funds throughout the EU, amounting to about one-half of the total (management) fee.[35] They are followed by money market funds, where they amount to 41% of the management fee (see Figure 5). Lower levels of retrocession fees have been charged by the hedge fund industry that, traditionally, charges high levels of management fees.[36]

Figure 5. Retrocession fee by country (as a % of management fee)

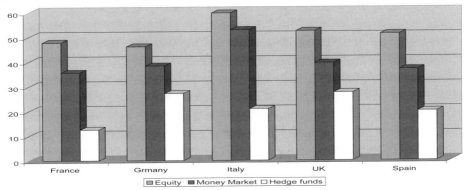

Source: ZEW/OEE.

The composition of commission fees varies widely from one country to another. In making a breakdown of the different costs charged by fund service providers in Europe, the following points need to be kept in mind:

- Price comparisons of services offered by funds are complicated by the fact that the data are not clearly comparable. In Spain, for example,

---

manufacturers with external ones, to induce external manufacturers to pay higher commissions and to become more efficient.

[34] This may change as a result of the implementation of MiFID, see chapter 4.

[35] For example, the retrocession fee amounts to 60%, 52%, 51%, 48% and 46% of the management fee in Italy, the UK, Spain, France and Germany, respectively.

[36] Hedge funds are the most expensive product in fund markets, charging from 1% to 3% as a management fee as well as a 20% performance fee.

the majority of funds are sold without a 'load fee', which explains why Spanish management fees are among the highest in Europe.

- Products and services often vary across countries and even among funds located in the same country. For example, the same fund could have a different price in relation to the destination because of different regulatory regimes and distribution structures. Prices could differ if the product is offered on a domestic or cross-border basis.

- Consumer behaviour and habits in different member states could differ significantly, thus determining the level of fees charged by funds. Strong differences emerge if one compares, for instance, UK investors, who are typically attentive observers of dynamic markets, with Italian or Spanish investors.

Bearing in mind these difficulties, a measure recommended by the European Commission to compare commission costs in different countries is the total expense ratio (TER), as shown in Figure 6. The TER is measured as the total cost faced by funds and it is equal to the ratio of total operational costs[37] faced by funds to the average of the net asset value (NAV).[38] Data show that between 2002 and 2005, the TER in Europe has increased by 0.06%.[39] It means that the rate of growth of operational cost is growing a little bit more than the Total Asset Value (TAV), which grew 74.5% between 2002 and 2005. The high level of operational costs is especially due to implicit fees which were higher than explicit fees. In fact, while the operational costs faced by a fund to invest its clients' money have basically remained the same, the remuneration paid to distributors has increased. Hence, the growth in TER is essentially explained by higher retrocession fees: due to higher costs in distribution services, funds tend to charge higher costs to end-investors.

---

[37] The 2004 Commission Recommendation, discussed in chapter 3 proposes to distinguish between explicit and implicit fees to include in the calculation of operational costs. Explicit fees are defined as the remuneration of fund managers for their services and costs incurred to run the business, while implicit fees include direct operating expenses, transaction fees and client transactions loads. Retrocession fees are part of the latter.

[38] When we use this value to refer to a country, it is expressed as total asset value (TAV).

[39] In the same period, the TER in the US decreased on average by 3.4% each year.

*Figure 6. Total expense ratios (TER), by country**

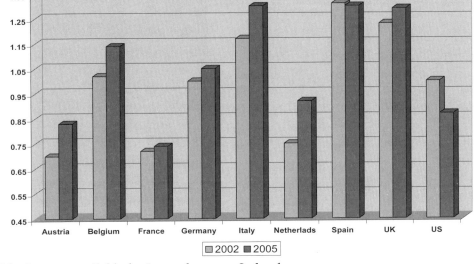

* No data are available for Luxembourg or Ireland.
Source: ZEW/OEE, ICI.

The most urgent issue to be addressed by the European asset management industry is how to secure an appropriate level of investor protection in a rapidly changing landscape. Under UCITS III, firms have gained the opportunity to use more advanced portfolio management techniques, but this should not bring about additional complexities for end-investors. It is to be welcomed indeed that investors have a broader choice among personalised and advanced financial products. This should, however, be accompanied by a more articulated disclosure.

The low level of transparency in the financial industry does not help investors. Funds do not disclose the implicit costs (principally retrocession fees and exit costs) and underperformance costs (resulting from unsuccessful stock selection decisions). Most funds do not follow the Commission recommendation regarding which costs should be included or excluded in the TER calculation. End-investors are thus left with an indicator that is inconsistently applied among firms, which is confusing. This emphasises again the problem of asymmetric information between the industry and end-investors. The situation becomes more difficult when comparing the TER applied to different products in different countries, because of the diversity in regulatory regimes.[40]

The above considerations give further evidence of the low levels of transparency of fund markets and of the need for a change. The Commission should therefore urgently consider how to arrive at a truly uniform TER for all European fund products. In addition, the industry could also take the initiative by adopting standards to ease the comparison of fund performance. The standard should allow for a single method for reporting, record-keeping and marketing of performance of investment managers. It should also facilitate market access for foreign investment management firms.[41]

In conclusion, the sale of sophisticated, alternative investment funds to mass-market investors has further increased the bargaining power of the financial institutions over investors. Financial institutions should consider more carefully the feeling of weakness on the part of their customers. They are the end-users of the products and the real judges of the financial stability. If a downturn starts (as has been the case since August 2007), European investors will be reluctant to believe in the soundness of European financial markets. As a consequence, in line with the irrational behaviour theory, they will start to sell their investment positions creating the basis for a period of market instability, leading to even more instability. Therefore, firms that want to preserve their businesses would be advised to consider their investors' needs as essential, rather than pursuing their own aims.

---

[40] It would be hard for investors to evaluate differences in savings products without the possibility to focus on the trade-off between price and quality, because there is almost no information about the precise value of the product.

[41] The Chartered Financial Analysts proposed 'Global Investment Performance Standards' (GIPS) as a harmonised way to measure investment performance in a fair and comparable way. The GIPS was adopted in 2005 and have been applicable since 2006.

3. THE 2002 UCITS AMENDMENTS AND THE ONGOING REVIEW

In regulatory terms, the asset management industry as such does not exist. Rather, the regulatory regime depends upon the particular license that the financial institution in question possesses. One may be licensed as an asset management company, a bank, an insurance company, a pension fund, a broker or an investment fund, which immediately raises the question of possible inconsistencies across regulatory regimes, duplication or arbitrage among regimes. For certain segments of the asset management business, the choice of regulatory regime will be non-existent, as they unambiguously fall into one of the aforementioned categories; for others, however, the vertical regulatory framework does not lend itself well to the range of activities they undertake. This is especially true of investment firms that may manufacture and distribute insurance, pensions and investment products, all the while conducting regular banking activities such as deposit-taking.

The diversity across the EEA of the regulatory framework governing the sector is striking. It reflects fundamental differences in consumer preferences, cultural habits and institutional heritage, and it explains the variation from one country to another in the relative importance of these various sectors as conduits of financial intermediation, as outlined in the first chapter. Although sectoral regulation has been harmonised to a large extent at the European level, implementation of EU rules may vary, with supervisory structures and practices continuing to differ from country to country. In this report we focus primarily on the UCITS investment fund regime, which is open to review, and its interaction with MiFID. But we will make reference to the treatment under other regimes, as necessary.

EU regulation governing the free provision of financial services in the asset management industry across borders under home country rules started with the UCITS Directive of 1985, which introduced harmonised product regulation at the EU level for investment funds that were allowed for cross-border sales under the UCITS passport. It was followed in the early 1990s with directives defining the terms under which the banking, insurance and investment services sectors could 'passport' their activities across the EEA on the basis of authorisation from their home state regulator. The UCITS Directive was amended and expanded in 2002 to become more of a horizontal asset management directive to reflect the increasing convergence of the core sectors of the financial services industry. An agreement was also reached in 2002 on the last outstanding piece of free provision of cross-border services regulation in the financial services sector, the pension funds directive. In the meantime, the new wave of the Financial Services Action Plan (FSAP) had started to come into effect, most importantly in the form of MiFID and the prospectus Directive.

In this chapter, we will review and assess the UCITS 2002 amendments, discuss the Commission's White Paper and related initiatives and assess the coherence of the EU's retail investment product regime.

3.1   UCITS II and III

The 1985 UCITS Directive opened the way for the cross-border sale of investment funds in the EU. Subject to some general criteria regarding authorisation, legal structure, investment policies and disclosure, units of open-ended funds that invest in transferable securities could be sold freely throughout the EU. Marketing and tax rules did not fall within the scope of this directive, which meant that they remained regulated by host-country regulators. Prospectuses had to be translated into the official language of the host country, for example, and local consumer protection regulation – often very different between countries – had to be respected. Nor did the directive harmonise the prudential requirements of the companies managing investment funds. For example, the directive did not set a minimum capital standard or solvency requirements. This was subsequently modified by the 2002 amendments.

The asset allocation rules of the UCITS I were essentially quantitative. UCITS funds could invest in a diversified portfolio of listed equity and debt securities, respecting the 5/10/40% rule: 5% limits apply for stock of a single body (which can be extended to 10% by the home country authorities), and an overall limit of 40% for the total of large single blocks of securities. A limit of 10% applied for non-listed securities. Exceptions applied for government or government-guaranteed paper. The limit applicable for investment in other funds was 5% of the whole portfolio, meaning that funds of funds were not permitted. Real estate and commodity funds were excluded from the directive, as were other alternative investments, including hedge funds and private equity, and money market instruments.

The 2002 UCITS amendments expanded the scope of activities that were possible under the UCITS I Directive. One directive (UCITS II or the Product Directive) widens the investment possibilities of funds to include instruments such as derivatives and allows for new forms of funds, such as funds of funds, money market funds, cash funds or index tracker funds. A second directive – UCITS III or the Management Directive – detailed minimum standards, including the introduction of a minimum level of own funds to be held by a fund management company for prudential purposes, and broadened the permissible activities of the fund management company. It also introduced a simplified prospectus, which provides for key factual information about a UCITS to be presented to investors in an accessible and uniform format. The deadline for implementation was August 2003, although existing UCITS could be 'grandfathered' for a further five years.

The most important achievement of the updated UCITS, albeit in theory, is the single license for fund management companies. The 1985 UCITS Directive did not grant the single passport to companies for the wider scope of their activities; it only related to the cross-border marketing of its units. The minimum harmonisation at company-level in the 1985 directive was very limited and, in this respect, it could be considered surprising that the UCITS I Directive was so successful. The UCITS III Directive grants the 'single license' to fund management companies in the broad sense of the word. It comprises not only the management of investment funds – i.e. the core services – but also other activities related to portfolio management, such as pension funds for individuals, investment advice, safekeeping (custody) and administration of investment funds, which are seen as non-core or ancillary.[42]

---

[42] Other forms of portfolio management, i.e. management of pension fund portfolios or those of individuals, are presented as a form of derogation from the

UCITS III, however, does not clearly distinguish between the responsibilities of the home and the host countries. The operating conditions of investment fund companies are set and monitored by *home* country authorities (Art. 5 to 5h). According to Art. 5h, which copies Art. 11 of the Investment Services Directive (ISD, 93/22/EEC), conduct of business rules are set by the home country. However, if the investment company provides the non-core or ancillary services, portfolio management, investment advisory services or custody, the conduct-of-business rules in force in the *host* member state shall apply (Art. 6b). The powers of the home member state are further undermined in Art. 6c, which grants powers to the host member states to impose their conduct of business rules, as well to funds sold by local branches or under the freedom to provide services. Moreover, the amendments left Art. 3 of the 1985 directive intact, which requires the management company to be located in the member state where the relevant UCITS is situated – thus preventing any possibility of a real Management Company Passport. This contradictory situation, and the existence of MiFID, are compelling reasons to review these provisions.

UCITS III also introduced a simplified prospectus for the sale of harmonised investment funds. Prospectus documentation needs to be composed of a full and a simplified prospectus, which must be kept up to date, and an annual and half-yearly report. All these documents need to be provided and published in the official language(s) of the host country but should allow for cross-border recognition without additional documents.[43] The notification and translation requirements of UCITS continue to vary from one member state to another, however. Although the directive specifies which documents need to be provided to the authorities, many countries require additional information, a fund's board minutes for

---

central objective of the directive, which is management of investment funds as authorised under the directive (Art. 5).

[43] For comparison, the prospectus directive regarding initial offerings of securities (2003/71/EC) proposes that only the summary note will have to be translated for cross-border offerings in case the registration document and securities note are published in a language that is "customary in the field of finance". In addition, UCITS III does not follow the maximum harmonisation approach of the prospectus directive.

example, which may also need to be translated.[44] Such requirements unnecessarily lengthen the registration period.

UCITS II determines what kind of funds can be sold with a single license and sets investment allocation rules. It now also covers funds invested in money market instruments, bank deposits, financial derivatives, index funds, units of other UCITS and non-UCITS funds (funds of funds). The investment limits of the 1985 directive have been further detailed, depending on the instruments. Overall, the 5/10/40% rule continues to apply. Maximum levels of 10% apply for investments in money market instruments issued by the same entity, and of 20% for investments in one single other UCITS (for funds of funds and index tracker funds or Exchange Traded Funds) and for deposits with credit institutions. Investments in non-UCITS are limited to 30% of the assets of the UCITS.

In 2007, the EU adopted an *implementing directive* (Directive 2007/16/EC) which expands the asset classes eligible for inclusion in UCITS funds. It concerns: asset backed securities, listed closed-end funds, Euro Commercial Paper, index-based derivatives and credit derivatives. This decision makes use of the limited (and only) 'comitology' provisions under UCITS I, which allows for clarifications to the definitions to be made via a simple decision taken in the European Securities Committee (the so-called 'level 2 Committee').[45]

The European Commission also adopted two *recommendations* in 2004 explaining its interpretation on the information to be provided in the simplified prospectus and on the use of financial derivative instruments in UCITS. The first recommendation sets common interpretations on the presentation and measurement of fund performance, subscription and redemption fees, soft commissions and fee-sharing arrangements (Commission Recommendation 2004/384/EC). The Commission recommended that a total expense ratio (TER) should be disclosed: the

---

[44] See Clifford Chance (2002), *Constraints on Marketing UCITS Cross-Border in Europe*, Summary Paper, 22 February.

[45] 'Comitology' provisions allow changes to be made to an EU measure without going through the formal EU decision-making process, but by the agreement of a specialised Committee. This only applies for those articles of a directive or regulation where this was foreseen in the original text.

expected cost structure, i.e. an indication of all costs applicable; all subscription and redemption charges and other expenses directly paid by the investor; an indication of all the other costs not included in the TER; and the portfolio turnover rate. Equally, it established that the existence of fee-sharing agreements and soft commissions must be disclosed. The second recommendation proposes a uniform understanding of risk measurement methodologies in the UCITS area with regard to derivative products (Commission recommendation 2004/383/EC).

In addition, the European Commission adopted an *interpretative communication* in 2007 on the respective powers of the home and the host member state in the marketing of UCITS, which tried to elaborate a common understanding on some unclear provisions of the UCITS III Directive discussed above (COM(2007)112). According to the European Commission's interpretation, home member states clearly have exclusive responsibilities under UCITS III, on which the host member states should not encroach. The residual host country competences are related to advertising, marketing and the distribution infrastructure as strictly related to UCITS. Host member state rules falling outside the scope of the directive are in any event harmonised at the EU level under MiFID and various marketing and consumer protection directives, according to the European Commission. This interpretative communication was adopted by the European Commission in March 2007, awaiting the results of the White Paper and the consultation process of the UCITS review.

3.2   Assessment

The 2002 amendments have further contributed to the growth of the UCITS brand. The impressive growth documented in chapter 1 was made possible by the changes discussed above, especially the expansion of the type of funds UCITS could invest in, such as index funds, derivatives and other non-UCITS funds. Exchange-traded funds, for example, have seen an impressive take-off in Europe, helped by the changes in UCITS II. Other changes, however, did not go far enough or did not succeed in their objective.

The simplified prospectus was supposed to be the information-dissemination instrument *par excellence*, and it was also intended to be a marketing tool. But in light of experience of past four years, it is clear that the simplified prospectus is anything but a marketing tool. Although originally intended as a document for retail investors, the simplified prospectus does not achieve its goal, because it is neither structured in a conducive format nor is it sufficiently harmonised. National requirements across the EEA on the simplified prospectus vary considerably, with some regulators taking a lax approach and certifying short and light documents, while others take a far more risk-averse stance, asking for more details and specifications, such that simplified prospectuses become far lengthier and more detailed than they were originally intended to be. Making the UCITS simplified prospectus more understandable for retail investors will not be an easy task, however.[46]

As touched upon above, one of the fundamental problems with the UCITS Directive resides in the non-harmonised rules for advertising and conduct of business in general. As it stands, the UCITS Directive leaves important scope for residual powers to be retained by host member states. Thus, the uneven playing field, as outlined in Arts 5 and 6 of the Management Passport Directive, is a source of confusion for investors and distorts competition. There would be considerable advantage to work within the framework of a harmonised set of rules not only for UCITS but also for all substitute products. To this effect, the representative of the Belgian supervisory authority CBFA subscribed to the recommendations of the Klinz report (see European Parliament, 2007) to find practical solutions to discrepancies in marketing rules and favoured a voluntary code of conduct by the industry.

As far as the scope for improving cross-border investment flows is concerned, the main impediments are the handicapped product passport (since marketing rules are not harmonised) and the inconsistent application of the notification procedure. The Committee of European Securities Regulators (CESR) has been working on a standard notification letter and official attestation, but more needs to be done, namely:

-   publication of national marketing requirements on the website of regulators, which should foster greater transparency and thereby drive down compliance costs;

---

[46] The following discussion is based upon the presentation by Greet T'Jonck, Deputy Director, Commission Bancaire, Financière et des Assurances (CBFA, Belgium) at the first meeting of the Task Force, 21 June 2006.

-   harmonisation of advertising rules and all residual competences that stay within the remit of host authorities;
-   clarification of the definition of "marketing" in section 8 of the UCITS Directive to ease the functioning of the product passport work;[47] and
-   harmonisation of conduct of business rules across the EU for UCITS, as was done in MiFID.

On the cross-border management of UCITS – the so-called 'Management Company Passport' – the requirement that UCITS must keep their head office in the same member state as the registered office is seen as a big obstacle (Art. 3). Moreover, the implementation of a true management company passport requires appropriate supervisory cooperation between two or more supervisory authorities. These two obstacles can be overcome by deleting Art. 3 and drafting a clear sharing of competences between the Management Company regulator and the UCITS regulator (with essential principles for cooperation at Level 1, and implementing measures at Level 2). Such articulated cooperation provisions have already been set up in the context of other directives (Banking Directives, MiFID, Market Abuse Directive), some of which have already been successfully tested in practice.

As regards the 'Product Directive', the maintenance of the quantitative asset allocation rules and restrictions on investments in various asset classes – as currently defined by the directive – seems anathema in the context of a multiplication of asset classes and new techniques adopted to manage risk in portfolios. The exercise of defining eligible assets and attempting to regulate investment risk for UCITS is seen to be outdated. It is neither sustainable given the existing institutional framework, nor does it adequately take account of the lessons of modern portfolio theory. The strict quantitative limits imposed on UCITS managers in their asset allocation strategies ought to be done away with altogether in favour of a risk-based approach, akin to the prudent man principle that prevails in managing the assets of pension funds. On the basis of simple examples of portfolio optimisation, it can be demonstrated that that there are clear situations in which regulating investment policies – on the choice of assets held by a UCITS as well as on quantitative investment limits –

---

[47] In this context, see the Commission's interpretative Communication on the residual host country powers, including marketing, quoted above (Com (2007) 112).

leads to worse outcomes for unit-holders. Arbitrary quantitative investment limits and restrictions on asset choice can actually reduce the range of possibilities for a fund manager to reduce risk through portfolio diversification, as well as leading to inferior risk-return profiles for these funds relative to those that would be managed under a risk-based approach to replace Art. 22 of the UCITS Directive. Indeed, the investment restrictions in Section V of the UCITS Directive could give investors a false sense of security: they do not in any way guarantee the quality of portfolio management (see Casey, 2006).

Sectoral and index tracker funds are other examples of the constraints imposed by quantitative restrictions, i.e. the 5/10/40% rule for UCITS. Many European sector-based indexes cannot be accurately tracked without exceeding the 40% rule. Some even exceed the 10% rule since there are not enough companies in a certain sector present in the index, or there are a few big firms dominating the sector, and thus the index (Lannoo, 2002).

In addition, there are institutional constraints that prevent rapid amendments to the UCITS Directive's rules on investment restrictions. Today, any changes that have to be made to these rules, in the absence of the full Lamfalussy framework, take at least two years, if not more. But even with a full Lamfalussy framework in place, it is not clear whether the exercise of defining eligible assets every three to four years makes much sense. As long as the 'product approach' prevails, the inevitable trade-off will be to balance the need of investment managers to have a regularly updated legislative framework that will allow them to invest in new ranges of financial assets, against the sheer cost in terms of public resources needed to go through the painstaking exercise of periodically updating the list of eligible assets (see Casey, 2006).

On the contrary, the example of the 130/30 funds indicates precisely how much can be done within the present framework. This strategy, which adopts hedge-fund based techniques, is to first put 130% into an index like the S&P 500 (by borrowing an additional 30% of the value of the fund's assets and investing them alongside), and then to sell short 30% in stocks expected to do worse than the market. Such strategies adopt 'shorting' for a limited portion of the portfolio since their computer-driven models can efficiently apply a broad range of analytical criteria – valuation, momentum, analyst sentiment and earnings quality, for example – to a whole universe of stocks. 130/30 funds are similar to long-only funds to the extent that they build a portfolio as normal, and have a net exposure of

100% of NAV to long positions (the additional 30% of NAV that is borrowed to increase exposure to long positions is effectively cancelled out by short sales to the tune of 30% of NAV). It is likely that these products will become increasingly appealing to retail investors in future, particularly given that they can be offered within a UCITS structure and could offer superior risk-adjusted performance relative to pure long-only funds. The common interpretation of UCITS rules only allows for synthetic shorting, that is achieving the same pay-off structures as short-selling via the use of derivatives, such as options and contracts for difference.[48]

Looking more broadly at the asset management industry, it is remarkable to see how much the approach differs across sectors (see Annex II). Asset allocation rules governing pension funds are the most liberal to be found at EU level. Pension funds are only subject to a very general prudent man principle in their asset allocation strategies. Insurance groups face quantitative minimum requirements, but these are in the process of being revised and liberalised in the context of the Solvency II exercise.

The Committee of European Securities Regulators (CESR) has examined the subject of eligible assets in the context of its expert group on investment management, more specifically, on the use of hedge fund indices as financial indices for the purpose of UCITS, and alternative investments.[49] It arrived at two principal observations:

1. Concerning alternative investments, it acknowledged that there are still difficulties in recognising their UCITS eligibility owing to the fact that the concept of hedge funds is still not well defined. The recent US experience attests to the difficulties and controversy of such an exercise, yet CESR nevertheless remains committed, at a minimum, to categorising different types of hedge funds to gain more clarity in definition for the purpose of UCITS investments.

2. How to see UCITS compared to other competing products? There is a high level of protection of investors, so the quality of the product is sound. A key point on alternative investments, especially related to the

---

[48] Taken from Andrew Collins, "130/30 Funds – A New Middle Ground", Fortis Prime Fund Solutions (available at www.aima.org).

[49] The following is based on a presentation by Carlo Comporti, Secretary General, Committee of European Securities Regulators (CESR), to the Task Force, 9 November 2006.

marketing and distribution of these products, is the industry's suggestion to use the MiFID framework for the distribution of these products without any further product regulation. But CESR is opposed to this idea for two reasons:

i) *Retail investor protection.* Distribution rules are too lax under MiFID for alternative investments to be marketed to retail investors without any further product regulation.

ii) Competitive effect. If alternative investments can be marketed to retail clients only on the basis of suitability/appropriateness, without additional protection, UCITS could effectively be driven out of the market.

It is difficult to see whether and how this will be enforced in practice by EU regulators, however, as they may apply different policies on the subject.

On the other hand, there is no need to package all investment funds as UCITS, which has essentially been designed with retail investors in mind. One must bear in mind, however, that due to the absence of a facilitating framework for cross-border sales in the institutional market, the UCITS market today is widely used as a vehicle for institutional funds. Indeed, the majority of the UCITS market today is accounted for by institutional funds. If the objective is to facilitate cross-border marketing and sales in the institutional space, other possibilities exist, such as the proposal for a pan-European private placement regime. A harmonised private placement regime could be put forward to enhance market efficiency for non-harmonised products without hurting retail investors, even though it is difficult to guarantee that no 'retail cascade', i.e. further dissemination to the public, would not occur in practice.[50] CESR could determine the criteria for eligible investors under this regime, which would benefit from a less restrictive regulatory environment than UCITS. But such

---

[50] Private placement is usually understood as a specific sales method for investment products. It is a (non-)regulated space where the buyer and seller can conduct transactions if they, their transaction and possibly the object of the deal comply with certain conditions. The regime itself then consists of a set of conditions market participants have to fulfil in order to benefit from a waiver of the requirements and rules that would apply in the event of public offerings, which fall under the prospectus directive (see European Commission, 2007d).

a private placement regime will work only if it is complemented by another EU legal action regarding the products to be sold: a private placement regime will only facilitate the offer of funds, in particular alternative investments – it may not ease the restrictions for institutional investors to invest in such funds. Therefore, as a necessary complement to an EU private placement regime, it is crucial to extend the UCITS Directive beyond the current scope of eligible assets, in order to ease the investment in alternative investments (hedge funds, funds of hedge funds, real estate funds, private equity funds) by institutional investors of many member states, which is not possible within the current regulatory framework.

3.3   The Commission's White Paper and draft release

Although the UCITS Directives had only been amended in 2001, the Commission acknowledged by 2006 that an additional review of the UCITS regime was required. The review was justified on several grounds, namely that the 2001 Product Directive (amended) was seen to be too prescriptive, UCITS were increasingly open to competition from other financial products and the introduction of MiFID posed particular challenges for the UCITS regime that had to be addressed. The White Paper did not call for a fundamental overhaul of the existing framework, but rather for a structured review of the need for changes to the scope and regulatory approach. The White Paper was followed by a draft release in March 2007, which outlined in detail the proposed changes to UCITS II and III.

The White Paper proposes a set of measures to improve the efficiency of the European fund industry, by making the single market for investment funds work as intended. To this effect, it proposes measures related to removing barriers related to cross-border marketing and fund distribution – e.g. via proposals on revising the simplified prospectus and accelerating the notification procedure – the facilitation of cross-border fund mergers and asset pooling, a real single management company passport and strengthened supervisory cooperation. Furthermore, amendments to the directive are needed to make the simplified prospectus work in practice. MiFID rules on inducements will have a significant impact on rendering the distribution system more transparent, as they stipulate that distribution fees can only be accepted from product providers if there is clear evidence this is in the interest of clients (in order to prevent a biased selection of products by distributors and biased advice within that selected panel of funds). In addition, the precise terms of these distribution agreements (or, at a minimum, their 'essential terms'), must be disclosed to clients prior to the service being delivered. On non-harmonised funds, the White Paper states that it is too early to table legislative proposals. The White Paper also announced that the European Commission would take an initiative on an EU-wide private placement regime to fill the lacuna of a European product for sophisticated investors. The initial orientations of possible adjustments to the UCITS Directive (European Commission, 2007b) go in the same direction as outlined in the White Paper.

The green light for the UCITS amendments was given by the May 2007 Ecofin Council, which stated that "the best approach at this stage consists in targeted amendments to the UCITS directives" and invited the European Commission to present proposals on the subject. In this regard, the Council emphasised the importance of consistency between MiFID and UCITS, and insisted on ensuring "in the context of retail distribution of, and advice on, UCITS, that all steps are taken by the Commission and the Member States in enforcing the conduct of business rules provided for in the MiFID, (...) and stresses the need for clearly ensuring the coherence of application of the MiFID and the UCITS directives." The Council further invited the Commission "to review the consistency of EU legislation regarding the different types of retail investment products (such as unit-linked life insurance, investment funds, certain structured notes and certificates), so as to ensure a coherent approach to investor protection and to avoid any mis-selling possibilities."

The same Ecofin Council meeting also discussed a common approach to hedge funds, and recommended the 'indirect supervision' approach, through close supervisory monitoring of credit institutions' exposures to hedge funds. The Council called upon creditors and investors to also examine whether the current level of transparency of hedge funds' activities is appropriate and requested the European Commission to take all these elements into accounts in the context of its work on the retail-oriented non-harmonised fund industry.

The White Paper is less clear on the degree to which the Lamfalussy procedure will be applied to UCITS. Although there seems to be a consensus that this should be done, it is not sure how far this will go. The question is also whether this can, in view of the comments made above, go far enough.

3.4   Coherence of the retail investment product regime in the EU

The major challenge for the years to come is to work out a coherent regime for retail investment products. Households are now faced with increasingly difficult investment choices that have ever more serious consequences in light of an ageing population and the increasingly obvious unsustainability of the pay-as-you-go pensions regime. Despite this backdrop, households are often ill-prepared to make well-informed choices on a self-directed basis, due to high levels of financial illiteracy.

A comparison of various national regimes within the EU covering retail investment products reveals an immense diversity, with a patchwork of different obligations on distributors regarding disclosure and investor protection, different forms of prudential supervision and a high degree of variation in marketing and advertising rules. The implementation of MiFID, with a far-reaching harmonisation of conduct of business rules, is triggering a horizontal review, which is accelerated by the ongoing UCITS review.[51]

An additional complexity is added to the exercise by the fact that many constituent elements of the retail investment product regime are shared competences between the EU, the member states and the industry, which militates against the emergence of a coherent framework. This problem is clearly stated in the 'Delmas-Marsalet report', a study that was commissioned by the French Minister of Finance to examine the issue (see AMF, 2005). It proposed a charter for the commercialisation of financial products, covering rules on client suitability and appropriateness, the impartiality of investment advice, the need to better educate and target consumers and the creation of a financial ombudsman. Properly addressing these concerns would require an extension of the MiFID regime to cover other investment products (such as unit-linked life insurance), cross-sectoral consistency of national implementation of EU legislation (as opposed to merely at the vertical directive level) and the elaboration of pan-European industry codes of conduct.

It is clear that the current EU framework governing retail investment products remains both primarily vertical, and incomplete (see Table 2). The

---

[51] See the Call for Evidence published by the European Commission (2007e) in October 2007.

level of mandatory fiduciary care afforded to retail investors as well as the level of supervision or oversight undertaken by regulatory authorities may vary depending on the distribution channel through which they access investment products, even if, in terms of outcomes or payoff profiles, the products are broadly similar. MiFID provides a detailed framework for ensuring a coherent approach to disclosure and point of sale regulation by investment firms for all financial instruments, including funds and structured notes. In addition, it includes rules on inducements which influence the remuneration structures that are permissible in the distribution of financial instruments. Nothing comparable exists today at European level for other products (although it may exist at national level). As regards insurance products, the Insurance Mediation Directive (2002/92/EC) only sets out basic requirements for insurance intermediaries to deliver advice, taking into account the demands and needs of the policy-holder. For other listed securities, the Prospectus Directive sets out detailed disclosure rules, but addresses marketing rules only to a very limited extent (e.g. the language regime). For private placements, the MiFID rules will apply, to the extent that the products are sold via banks, brokers or financial advisers licensed under this directive. For expert investors and large undertakings, a lighter regime may apply.

Table 2. EU regulatory framework for retail investment products (long-term)

Product / Regime	UCITS	Non-UCITS (i.e. hedge funds)	Life-insurance products	Listed security	Un-listed security
Marketing rules	Local rules/ MiFID	(MiFID)	Insurance Mediation Directive	Prospectus Directive (part)	(MiFID)
Disclosure	UCITS/ MiFID	MiFID	Life Insurance and Insurance Mediation Dir.	Prospectus Directive	MiFID
Asset allocation rules	UCITS	–	Life Insurance Directive	–	–
Prudential rules	UCITS/ MiFID/ CRD	MiFID/ CRD	Life Insurance Directive	–	–

The EU Finance Ministers Council is thus right to ask for a review of the consistency of the EU legislative framework for retail investment products. In view of the short description above, however, elaborating a more coherent regime will be a complex exercise. A harmonised regime for private placements, on which the European Commission is consulting, would be a step forward towards more consistency, but it would at the same time reinforce the vertical structure of the regulatory framework, and not necessarily strengthen the overall coherence of the retail investment product regime. Some products would thus be tightly regulated at EU level, whereas for others, there would only be general service level regulation. The problems raised by the interaction of a product directive (UCITS) with a services (MiFID) directive, discussed in the next chapter, indicate that many questions remain to be answered.

4. MiFID's Impact on the Fund Management Industry

There remains considerable uncertainty as to how exactly the MiFID and UCITS Directives will interact in the long run. This state reflects the growing pains of a regulatory transformation that represents no less than a tectonic shift from intense and prescriptive product regulation to a more flexible, principles-based regulation of management functions. Unlike UCITS, MiFID is a horizontal directive that cuts across the entire financial services industry (except for insurance). Precisely because the two directives are rooted in diverging regulatory philosophies, they are not natural partners, and the exercise of trying to fit the two together will likely be neither effortless nor seamless.

The confusion can be traced to apparently contradictory at first sight, or, in the least, ambiguous, wording in MiFID as to how its provisions relate to collective investment schemes. In reality, the UCITS-MiFID nexus is a web of dizzying complexity, on which this chapter attempts to shed more light. On the one hand, MiFID Recital 15 and Art. 2(1)(h) state that collective investment schemes (whether or not coordinated at EU level), their management companies and depositaries are excluded from the scope of MiFID provisions. Since UCITS are collective investment undertakings that are coordinated at Community level, they, their managers and depositaries do not come under MiFID rules.

On the other hand, UCITS are listed in Section C of MiFID Annex I as MiFID financial instruments. Therefore, in their dealings with clients involving transactions in UCITS, all MiFID firms must apply conduct of business rules, which include best execution and suitability.[52] Yet conduct of business rules do not apply to eligible counterparties, otherwise known as 'per se financial institutions'. And MiFID Art. 24(2) binds member states' competent authorities to recognize as eligible counterparties UCITS and their management companies, meaning that in their transactions with investment firms, they are by default not afforded conduct of business protections. However, investment managers (including UCITS) can request under the same article to have their transactions protected by MiFID's conduct of business rules, including best execution.

In addition, despite the Art. 2(1)(h) exemption, MiFID Art. 66 brings some UCITS management company functions under the scope of MiFID (see Table 3). Thus, UCITS management companies are subject to both the UCITS and MiFID Directives: when providing ancillary investment services (investment advice, individual portfolio management, etc.) they are governed by MiFID, whereas the UCITS Directive covers the designation of management companies. Under the original UCITS Directive, management companies could only provide collective investment services. But under the 'product directive' component of UCITS III, the range of services management companies could provide were extended to cover individual portfolio management, allowing them to compete directly with portfolio managers, who carry out these activities under a MiFID license.[53] The decision to apply certain conduct of business rules to UCITS management companies that are undertaking individual portfolio management was a necessary consequence of the wider powers given to managers of UCITS under UCITS III: its purpose was to ensure that a level playing field emerges in the management of individual portfolios, whether by MiFID-authorised investment managers or UCITS management companies.

---

[52] The classification of UCITS under Art. 19(6) as a 'non-complex' financial instrument by default means it can be exempted from the appropriateness test in Art. 19(5) for execution-only transactions.

[53] FSA (2006), DP06/03: Implementing MiFID's best execution requirements, May, p. 20, which cites Art. 5(3) of the UCITS Directive, as amended by Directive 2001/107/EC.

Table 3. MiFID provisions that apply to UCITS

MiFID provisions apply to UCITS management companies *only* when they provide the following services:	MiFID provisions that apply to UCITS management companies:
<ul><li>Discretionary portfolio management</li><li>Investment advice</li><li>Custody and administration</li></ul>	<ul><li>Dealings as counterparty to public authorities (Art. 2.2)</li><li>Cross-border takeover of a company (Art. 10(4)) if it leads to a qualifying holding in that firm</li><li>Capital requirements (Art. 12)</li><li>Organisational requirements (Art. 13) (in particular conflicts of interest)</li><li>Conduct of business obligations (Art. 19) (in particular suitability and best execution)</li></ul>

The interaction between UCITS and MiFID is further complicated by the Art. 3(1) exemption, which leaves the decision to the discretion to individual EU member states whether to apply MiFID to legal persons who only receive/transmit orders in UCITS, who do not hold any clients' funds and who only carry out transactions with certain counterparties. Because these various options and possible exemptions raise serious concerns for a level playing field at the pan-European level, it would be sensible for the European Commission to clarify to what degree UCITS funds would potentially be affected by the Art. 3(1) carve-out (exemption).

The various layers of interaction, options and carve-outs described above paint a complex picture of the MiFID-UCITS nexus. Its more precise articulation over time will result in a robust learning-by-doing exercise for market participants and regulators alike. It will likely involve hiccoughs along the way. The Asset Management Sector Leader of the FSA, Dan Waters, playing on a phrase coined by the former US Secretary of Defense, has described the interaction between the UCITS and MiFID Directives as being "…full of both known unknowns and unknown unknowns."[54] His is a not so subtle recognition that regulators just as much as market

---

[54] "Opening up European markets for fund distribution: The impact of MiFID on UCITS distribution", speech by Dan Waters, Asset Management Sector Leader, FSA, City & Financial Croup Conference, London, 18 January 2007.

participants have yet to come to a better understanding of how the two directives will fit together in practice.

Table 4. Provisions that apply to UCITS: MiFID or member state discretion

UCITS funds	MiFID	Member state discretion
Fund distribution undertaken by an investment firm	X	
Fund distribution undertaken by fund management company		X
Fund distribution undertaken neither by a UCITS management company nor a MiFID investment firm		X
Investment advice on collective investment scheme given by investment firm	X	
Advice relating exclusively to collective investments given by fund management company		X
Advice on collective investments combined with other instruments given by the fund management company	X	
Advice on collective investment that is part of a package or a 'wrap'	X	
Reception/transmission of orders relating to collective investments only		X
Self-managed UCITS, distribution and advice		X (?)

At the same time, these differences are in many respects technical and touch only a few areas, and they therefore do not mean that UCITS and MiFID are fundamentally incompatible. At a very high level and overlooking some of the technical points where the fit is not perfect, the boundary between UCITS and MiFID is fairly clear. While UCITS governs the constitution, management, administration and process around the launch of a fund, MiFID governs commercial agreements between providers and distributors, as well as services related to distribution (e.g. brokerage and advice). As mentioned above, there are however a few important exceptions from this stylised picture, as follows:

1.   Where UCITS market their own funds or delegate this activity to an agent.

2. Execution – the boundary between UCITS and MiFID is not explicitly clear with regard to rules surrounding execution: the subscription/redemption of units in UCITS is governed by the UCITS Directive, while the reception/transmission of client orders in UCITS is governed by MiFID.

3. Where UCITS management companies carry out individual portfolio management in addition to their core activity of collective investment management.

The importance of getting these points resolved quickly should not be underestimated. If – as the current legislative framework seems to suggest – UCITS management companies can market and sell their funds cross-border under the UCITS rules, without being subjected to the MiFID regime, which applies when MiFID investment firms distribute those same funds, there is a fundamental incoherence in the regulatory architecture governing the marketing and selling of UCITS. In addition, there is evidence that member states are moving to address this disconnect in an uncoordinated manner, which could fragment the UCITS market. While some member states are deciding to impose MiFID rules on their own management companies or on foreign ones when they sell cross-border into their jurisdictions, others do not.

4.1   Uneven playing fields?

The degree of confusion prevailing among both regulators and market participants is worrisome to the extent that it could bring about further compliance, administrative and IT costs for the industry, as well as stifle innovation in both product development and in the evolution of the industry architecture (models of distribution, outsourcing, etc.) through continued regulatory uncertainty. In addition, the same options and exemptions mentioned above, which are the source of the confusion as to how MiFID and UCITS will interact, raise serious concerns about whether a level playing field will exist in the European investment management business post-MiFID.

Broadly speaking, there are five areas where MiFID impacts most on the asset management business: best execution, outsourcing, product fact disclosures, conflicts of interest and inducements. To the extent that some actors in the UCITS market face MiFID best execution rules that are considerably stricter than those under the UCITS Directive governing actors in the same market raises legitimate concerns about a distorted playing field.

Best execution

Concerning best execution, the investment management industry does not come under a harmonised set of rules, since some entities will fall under the light-touch UCITS regime for execution (taken from Art. 11 of the Investment Services Directive on conduct of business, which only sets out very high level principles), and others will be subjected to MiFID's more detailed rules on execution.[55] More precisely, management companies executing transactions in the process of managing collective investments do not come under MiFID's onerous best execution rules. They do when providing individual portfolio management services. The European Commission has clearly stated that where a UCITS management company outsources the management of a UCITS to an investment firm under Art. 5(g) of the UCITS Directive, the investment firm must give the UCITS conduct of business protections and treat it as a professional or retail client.[56] However, where the management company retains investment management functions and transacts with investment firms, it is to be considered an eligible counterparty, in line with MiFID Art. 24(2).

Broadening the debate beyond UCTIS, the French market regulator (Autorité des Marchés Financiers), has already declared its misgivings about the uneven application of best execution requirements among management companies: "As regards the best execution requirement, non-uniform treatment of management companies subject to MiFID in respect of all or part of their business and management companies not subject to

---

[55] Specifically, the requirements call for implementation of an execution policy and ongoing monitoring of execution quality delivered by the various regulated markets, MTFs and brokers used, based on the execution factors which the firm prioritises. In order to make the review of execution policy effective, firms will have to come up with metrics to quantify, or at least make a credible qualitative assessment of, execution quality. This exercise is particularly difficult for execution factors that are not easily quantifiable, such as likelihood of execution, market impact, etc.

[56] See the European Commission's FAQ on MiFID, Question 97 (http://ec.europa.eu/internal_market/securities/isd/questions/index_en.htm).

MiFID (those that manage only non-UCITS or only UCITS, for example), seems hard to justify."[57]

Outsourcing

The emphasis on fund management companies in the various MiFID exemptions and UCITS revision leaves one to wonder where and under what conditions self-managed UCITS fall under the MiFID umbrella. Under the UCITS Directive, both fund management companies and self-managed funds (e.g. SICAVs) may delegate investment management, administration and distribution functions to third-party service providers. In the case of delegation of the distribution, which set of rules prevails – those of UCITS or of MiFID?

Fact disclosures

Under UCITS Art. 28, UCITS management companies must disclose entry and exit commissions as well as other expenses or fees. The Commission's 2004 Recommendation encouraged member states to require UCITS to publish in the simplified prospectus total expense ratios (TERs) in order to better reflect the total operating costs of the fund.[58] However, the non-binding nature of the Recommendation means that member states have introduced different forms of TERs, making cross-border comparisons of costs difficult. MiFID also requires disclosure of costs and associated charges under Art. 19(3). To the extent that Art. 34(2) of the MiFID Implementing Directive[59] considers the simplified prospectus to be sufficient information for the purposes of MiFID Art. 19(3), MiFID firms which distribute UCITS will import the uneven application of disclosure of costs and charges that result from the patchy implementation of the Commission's 2004 Recommendation. In addition, level playing field issues are raised by Recital 55 of the MiFID implementing directive. Notwithstanding Art. 34(2) of the same directive, Recital 55 requires investment firms distributing units in UCITS to additionally inform their

---

[57] AMF (2006), Consultation on enforcing the best-execution principles in MiFID and its implementing directive, 25 July (http://www.amf-france.org/documents/general/7274_1.pdf).

[58] Commission Recommendation 2004/384/EC of 27 April 2004.

[59] Directive 2006/73/EKE.

clients about all the other costs and associated charges related to their provision of investment services in relation to units in UCITS. It is unclear how these disclosures are to be made, or what information precisely is required, leaving scope for divergent interpretations at the national level.

Conflicts of interest

As with best execution, the UCITS requirements on conflicts of interest are lighter than those of MiFID. The core duty of care to clients, which is the backbone of MiFID conduct of business rules, is given in Art. 19 (1), which requires investment firms, when providing investment services and/or, where appropriate, ancillary services to clients, to "act honestly, fairly and professionally in accordance with the best interests of its clients". Similarly, the UCITS Directive sets forth comparable requirements for collective investment management.[60] Notably, Art. 5h, Directive 2001/107/EC lists a set of principles a management company shall respect (taken from the ISD): i) acting honestly and fairly in conducting its business activities in the best interests of the UCITS it manages and the integrity of the market; ii) acting with due skill, care and diligence, in the best interests of the UCITS it manages and the integrity of the market; iii) trying to avoid conflicts of interests and, when they cannot be avoided, ensuring that the UCITS it manages are fairly treated; and iv) complying with all regulatory requirements applicable to the conduct of its business activities so as to promote the best interests of its investors and the integrity of the market. To give effect to these provisions, a UCITS management company must be "structured and organised in such a way as to minimise the risk of UCITS' or clients' interests being prejudiced by conflicts of interest between the company and its clients, between one of its clients and another, between one of its clients and a UCITS or between two UCITS".[61]

MiFID, on the other hand, requires firms to "maintain and operate effective organisational and administrative arrangements with a view to taking all reasonable steps designed to prevent conflicts of interest from

---

[60] See Art. 10 (2), UCITS I Directive 85/611/EEC: "The management company must act independently and solely in the interest of the unit-holders"; and Art. 5h of UCITS III Directive 2001/107/EC.

[61] UCITS III Directive 2001/107/EC, Art. 5f (1) (b).

adversely affecting the interests of its clients".[62] Where firms are not satisfied that the controls they have put into place around a conflict are sufficient to manage it, they must disclose the conflict to clients. In addition, they must maintain a register of those conflicts of interest, including potential conflicts, which they have identified as giving rise to potential client detriment. Those registers of conflicts, as well as their attendant controls, must be reviewed occasionally by the firm. This all means that the administrative requirements around the management of conflicts of interest are significantly more burdensome for MiFID-authorised firms, as opposed to those authorised under UCITS. While this will not necessarily lead to inefficiencies (given the stylised picture given above of MiFID as regulation distribution and UCITS the manufacturing and management of funds), it could lead to arbitrage where firms conduct activities that are fall in the UCITS-MiFID grey zone.

Inducements

MiFID takes a very strict stance on inducements, with a view to forcing more transparency in the market for the distribution of retail investment products, and to removing biases in investment advice that arise from product providers paying distributors a commission. The starting point is that inducements are banned, unless they meet the strict criteria laid out in Art. 26 of the MiFID Level 2 implementing directive. Firms can only receive fees, commissions or non-monetary benefits in relation to services provided to clients in the following cases:

- when the commissions/benefits are paid or provided to or by the client (or by a person acting on his behalf);
- when the commissions/benefits are paid or provided to or by a third party (or by a person acting on his behalf) if two cumulative sub-conditions are fulfilled: disclosure of such commissions/benefits to the client plus a need for enhancing the quality of the service through the payment of the commission; and
- when the commissions are necessary for the provision of the services and cannot give rise to conflicts of interest for ensuring acting in the best interests of the client.

---

[62] See MiFID, Art. 13 (3).

These provisions might create difficulties for widely accepted distribution practices in the fund management industry, namely the retrocession of fees from product providers to distributors, as described in chapter 2. In particular, in some instances product providers and intermediaries (which are not in the same immediate parent company) may be contemplating significant up-front payments as a condition for the provider's products being placed on, or even considered for, the intermediary's panel or recommended list. These payments would be unconnected with, and additional to, conventional commissions which would be paid on the sale of particular products. Such payments would not be consistent with the standards of conduct for firms – irrespective of whether they will be 'whole of market' or 'multi-tied'. Such introductory payments are thus incompatible with the fundamental principle that a firm must not conduct business under arrangements that might give rise to a conflict with its duty to customers.

Where UCITS are distributed by MiFID firms, the latter will have to comply with the rules on inducements. Because UCITS management companies are allowed to distribute third party funds under the Management Company Directive (at least according to CESR's interpretation), it was considered necessary to extend MiFID rules on inducements to cover the remuneration agreements struck between UCITS management companies and the fund management groups whose funds they may distribute in addition to their own, precisely in order to ensure that the playing field would be level.

How exactly the complex interaction between the UCITS and MiFID Directives plays out in practice will therefore have an important impact on the European fund industry, not least because UCITS constitute the vast majority of funds in the EU. This interaction is further complicated by the very real possibility that MiFID will be applied and interpreted differently in the various EU member states, meaning that the way MiFID and UCITS interact is also likely to vary from one member state to another. In reality, the potential impact of MiFID on the asset management industry, especially on distribution, could well reach far beyond what anyone had anticipated, or indeed, the European Commission intended.

Box 2. Substantive references to UCITS and collective investments in the MiFID Directive (2004/39/EC) and Implementing Directive

Recital 15 and Art. 2(1)(h) – Collective investment undertakings, whether coordinated at the EU level (i.e. UCITS) or not, together with their managers and depositaries do not fall under the scope of MiFID.

Art. 3(1) – Member States can decide whether or not to apply MiFID to legal persons who only receive/transmit units in collective investment undertakings and who do not hold any clients' funds and only transact with certain counterparties.

Art. 10(4) – Cross-border acquisitions by UCITS management companies that would result in a 'qualifying holding' (defined in MiFID Art. 4 (27) are subject to Art. 60, which relates to the consultations among the different competent authorities of the member states prior to the authorisation of cross-border business.

Art. 19(6) – Because UCITS is qualified as a non-complex instrument, investment firms do not need to apply the appropriateness test mentioned in Art. 19(5) when on an execution-only basis.

Art. 24(2) – UCITS and their management companies must be recognised as eligible counterparties by member states' regulatory authorities, which means MiFID's conduct of business rules do not apply for these transactions. However, this does not preclude them from requesting to opt-down (higher standard of investor protection) to a lower classification for the purposes of seeking protection under conduct of business rules.

Art. 66 – Certain MiFID articles will apply to UCITS management companies, including capital requirements, organisational requirements and conduct of business rules (see Table 2 above).

Recital 55 (Implementing Directive 2006/73/EC) – Although Art. 34 of Directive 2006/73/EC states that the simplified prospectus is enough for the purposes of Directive 2004/39/EC, investment firms distributing units in UCITS should additionally inform their clients about all the other costs and associated charges related to their provision of investment services in relation to units in UCITS.

Art. 34(2) (Implementing Directive 2006/73/EC) – The simplified prospectus is sufficient information for the purposes of MiFID Art. 19(3) on disclosing costs and charges associated with investing in a fund.

4.2   Further impact of MiFID on the asset management sector

The practical consequences of the application of the MiFID regime to UCITS might become very burdensome for UCITS management companies. As soon as they develop the MiFID services mentioned above, they will have to comply with a comprehensive set of rules regarding their organisation and functioning, and will still have to comply with the UCITS Directive provisions regarding their core activity of UCITS fund management. One can identify at least six areas of impact for those services, apart from collective portfolio management.

1.   Many functions have to be organised in an independent way (e.g. compliance function, risk management and internal audit). Although MiFID provides that this requirement can be softened or exempted with a proportionality test (for SMEs in particular), some of these exemption cases will be offered only if the management company is able to prove that it fulfilled the conditions to be exempted.

2.   The restrictions and internal disclosure of personal transactions of management companies' staff is regulated in detail by MiFID. This might raise concerns, since, for instance, the scope of relevant persons is now extended to relatives (including partners for instance) and professional relations. Regarding relatives, we do not know yet how member states will be able to strike the right balance between this requirement and the European and national obligations on data protection (which have to be applied for the MiFID transposition – see Recital 43 of Level 1 MiFID). In addition, those transactions will have to be disclosed 'promptly' (Art. 12 (b)), which might create some difficulties of organisation in the daily work of compliance officers of management companies.

3.   The management companies will have to deal not only with actual conflicts of interest but also with potential ones (Art. 21 Level 2 MiFID). It might raise difficulties since by their nature some conflicts of interest are not always easy to anticipate.

4.   The files of clients of management companies will have to be reclassified since MiFID introduces a distinction between eligible counterparts, professional clients and retail clients. But the question of a grandfathering clause for the treatment of existing clients' files (requiring or not new information today for already existing clients' files) is not answered by the MiFID.

5. Regarding best execution, even though this full requirement is only imposed on investment firms executing the transactions themselves (in general, the brokers), management companies will have to comply with it in the following way. When management companies provide individual portfolio management services or for the service of reception/transmission of orders, they have to transmit the orders to brokers for execution. MiFID requires management companies to provide for a 'transmission policy' that ensures that brokers have been selected by the management companies among those presenting the objective criteria of offering a high probability of best execution of orders. It means that management companies will not be responsible for the best execution of orders in practice as those orders are executed by the brokers, but that they will have to justify the way they have established their 'transmission policy'.

4.3   MiFID and the distribution of non-harmonised products

Much of the debate surrounding the Commission's work on the Green and White Papers has focused on eligible assets – i.e. which instruments could eventually be regarded as suitable for inclusion in a UCITS portfolio and which can not. The advantage of having a product that is harmonised at the European level like UCITS is that these funds can be marketed across the EU on the basis of a single document, the simplified prospectus, and under a single set of rules, which is not the case for non-harmonised funds.

With the proliferation of financial instruments, there has been significant pressure on the Commission (and CESR by extension) to widen the definition of eligible assets (which is the only way to widen the range of products that can be included in a UCITS without necessitating changes to the existing legislative framework). This pressure also arises from the fact that the market for UCITS, while originally designed essentially for retail investors, is today permeated with institutional players who seek to piggy-back on the passport for a 'retail' product as the only means to efficiently market a fund cross-border, even in the institutional space. In this respect, there have been and continue to be attempts to 'shoe-horn' various alternative products into UCITS, even though they may not be a particularly good fit for retail investors. This reality will necessitate a careful balancing act for regulators between on the one hand preserving the standard of investor protection for which UCITS is known, and on the other hand making the brand flexible enough to respond to ever greater competitive pressures in the global fund market – at least until a pan-European private placement regime and a light-touch harmonised regime for the treatment of non-UCITS funds, is in place.

The problem with trying to shoe-horn different products into the UCITS framework is that the exercise of defining eligible assets for UCITS is outdated. It is neither sustainable given the existing institutional framework, nor does it adequately take account of the lessons of modern portfolio theory.[63] Critics will contend however that it is precisely this measured consideration of eligible instruments that has established UCITS' reputation for ensuring a high degree of investor protection.

On the other hand, from an industry perspective, the accelerated pace of financial innovation means that the exercise of reconsidering which instruments are suitable for UCITS is handicapped by the slow legislative machinery and therefore not conducive to facilitating a competitive EU fund market. The industry sees a distinct possibility in MiFID to by-pass this bottleneck. The Commission's expert groups on alternative investments have recommended that alternative investment funds (e.g. hedge funds) be distributed to retail investors on a cross-border basis on the basis of MiFID's distribution framework without imposing any additional product or management regulation at EU level.[64] In other words, this suggestion would amount to a pure mutual recognition regime for alternative investment funds without any minimal level of harmonisation at EU level of the product. This is rather wishful thinking in light of the 40 years' EU experience with single market legislation (historical precedent shows that without a minimum degree of harmonised legislation at EU level, a single market cannot emerge).

In addition to the unrealistic ambition of a pure mutual recognition regime (i.e. one where there is no minimal product harmonisation at EU level), one has to consider whether regulators would really accept to passport an alternative investment fund across the EU without any form of pan-European product regulation. The answer from CESR is very clear:

---

[63] See Casey (2006).

[64] See Recommendations 1 and 4 of the Report of the Alternative Investment Expert Group: Managing, Servicing and Marketing Hedge Funds in Europe, European Commission (2006c).

impossible.[65] CESR's objections are based upon two grounds. First, retail investor protection: in CESR's view, distribution rules are simply too lax under MiFID for alternative investments to be marketed to retail investors without any further product regulation. Second, the competitive effect: if alternative investments can be marketed to retail clients only on the basis of MiFID suitability/appropriateness tests, the playing field in the European fund market would be severely distorted to the advantage of alternative funds.

UCITS is widely seen to be a major success story in Europe, the only example of a truly successful pan-European retail market for financial services to date. Today, it is a globally-recognised brand that is synonymous with investor protection and sound product quality. This success should be built upon, rather than undermined. No doubt markets move fast and the existing regulatory framework ought to reflect these changes. It is necessary, for example, to examine whether the quality of UCITS is indeed consistently superior on average (in terms of risk-return profiles) to that of alternative investment funds, on which no clear-cut answer has been given so far, although the inclusion of some portion of derivative instruments seems to have made a positive impact (European Commission, 2008). If not, there would be little reason to object to the wider inclusion of complex instruments in UCITS – under a Lamfalussy approach in order to allow for a frequent updating of eligible assets, following financial innovation. But at the same time, one must be aware that confidence in the widely-recognised UCITS label could be easily destroyed: building the trust and confidence of (international) investors in certain products takes years, and clumsy action by regulators could destroy this confidence overnight. That's why another route could be explored: to add a 'non-UCITS' part to the UCITS Directive. The latter solution would bring the advantage of setting up a new, complementary brand: the 'alter-UCITS' brand, which might become as successful as the UCITS one in the future.

The continuing uneven playing field between various savings products is therefore very worrying. Relying on MiFID alone for the distribution of alternative investment funds to a retail market audience without any additional product regulation would only exacerbate the problem. Indeed, the possibility for distributors to market an alternative

---

[65] For a more detailed view, see CESR (2006).

investment fund across the EU under the MiFID distribution passport but without the attendant UCITS product passport would undermine the very *raison d'être* of the UCITS brand – a high level of investor protection through a combination of product regulation and management regulation – effectively driving UCITS out of the market. As a consequence, vigilance and careful reflection are required on the part of regulators as they determine how exactly the MiFID distribution passport will apply to alternative investment funds, and whether this application is compatible with the UCITS Directive.

Currently, there is significant confusion in the marketplace as to how alternative investments will fit into the already tense MiFID-UCITS interaction. Under MiFID, it is not sure that a product has to be harmonised at the European level to enjoy pan-European distribution. All that is required for the (advised) sale of MiFID financial instruments is the suitability test and an appropriateness test for execution-only transactions (except under certain conditions). This looser regulatory framework (in the sense that MiFID does not regulate products) might apply not only to alternative investment funds, depending on how MiFID is ultimately interpreted, but also to structured product wrappers around these investments.

The case for the 'MiFID-isation' of alternative funds is less robust than for structured products. For example, even if EU regulators were to prevent the cross-border distribution of non-harmonised alternative investment funds, it is well possible that investment firms could offer through their branches in different EU member states a composite portfolio of structured products that are designed in-house (and therefore harmonised internally group-wide) to retail investors under MiFID distribution rules. This composite portfolio of structured products could be built through the (advised) sales of individual products that together form a portfolio akin to a fund in terms of diversification, etc. To the extent that composite portfolios made up of a combination of structured products or complex MiFID financial instruments can replicate UCITS risk-return profiles, and advised sales of these individual products (or as a package) can be done on a cross-border basis without any further product regulation, they have a significant advantage over UCITS in terms of the regulatory framework. So long as these products can be considered 'transferable securities' under MiFID, they qualify for pan-European distribution under the MiFID passport without further product regulation.

This possibility will *require a review by the Commission into the definition of 'transferable securities'*, which currently could be taken to mean various structured products under Art. 4(1)(18)b, which mentions "bonds or other forms of securitized debt". This definition could potentially include CDOs, CLOs, and various derivatives thereof. *Without a more precise definition of the term 'transferable securities', the UCITS market faces a severe threat from a new range of structured products.*

Another important question in the debate on the MiFID-isation of alternative investment funds and products relates to whether financial advisors are sufficiently competent to handle complex instruments and non-harmonised funds without the end-investor enjoying any kind of additional protection in the form of product regulation. There are good reasons to doubt this to be the case. Additionally, one must consider whether Independent Financial Advisers or ill-trained personnel at the point of sale in bank branches will really be capable of keeping pace with and understanding the vast influx of complex new products sufficiently well to act as the ultimate safeguard of investor well-being in a world devoid of product regulation. Will there not likely be a significantly enhanced risk of mis-selling under such circumstances? For this reason, any move away from product regulation must be accompanied by rigorous exercises to ensure sales forces are trained and competent to give advice on these products and are treating customers fairly.

In our view, MiFID should not be seen to grant a passport to the cross-border distribution to retail investors of any or all non-harmonised collective schemes and structured products with alternative investments as underlyings. But as it currently stands, it remains unclear whether or how regulators will prevent alternative investments from being distributed cross-border to a retail audience under MiFID. It is therefore essential that a proper articulation is developed of how MiFID applies to the cross-border sale of non-harmonised products as soon as possible. How broad a reading of MiFID is adopted by the Commission and national regulatory bodies will be critical to determining the future success of UCITS as a brand.

It is also useful to highlight how, in some member states, insurance products, some of which (e.g. unit-linked) can compete directly with UCITS without a similar degree of harmonised regulation, also (currently) enjoy a skewed playing field. One of the main causes of the unequal playing field between products is the differing conditions for the oversight and control over marketing documents for 'financial products' and 'insurance products'.[66] We are of the opinion that the exclusion of insurance products from the scope of MiFID does not make any sense. The comparable rules under the EU's Insurance Mediation Directive (2002/92/EC) are not comparable to the regime that MiFID has brought in place. The demand of the Ecofin Council, discussed in the previous chapter, to review the consistency of the EU's retail investment product regime so as to ensure a coherent approach to investor protection and to avoid any mis-selling possibilities, fits with this concern.

Box 3. Critical questions on the 'MiFID-isation' of non-harmonised products

- Is it advisable or desirable for investment firms to be able to distribute non-harmonised products cross-border to retail investors without any form of underlying product regulation at EU level?

- Are financial advisors capable of keeping pace with the vast influx of complex new products and competent enough to understand their inherent risks and correlations of risk with other financial instruments? Can financial advisors really be expected to be reasonable substitutes for EU-wide product regulation as the ultimate guardians of investor protection?

- Should the 'MiFID-isation' of alternative investment funds and other non-harmonised products be applicable for distribution to high net worth individuals only?

- Should there be an explicit European-wide definition of a high net worth individual to allow such a distribution framework? (There already is an implicit such definition in MiFID. One of the quantitative minimum thresholds for individuals to be classified as professional investors for the purposes of the applicability of conduct of business rules under MiFID is an individual who has a portfolio worth at least €500,000).

- How broadly can the term 'transferable securities' be interpreted? Further clarification on the nature of closed-ended funds that are eligible for UCITS under Art. 2 of Directive 2007/16/EC would be welcome.

---

[66] See the Delmas-Marsalet report (AMF, 2005) on the marketing of financial instruments, p. 18.

REFERENCES

AMF (Autorité des Marchés Financiers) (2005), Rapport relatif à la commercialisation des produits financiers (rapport Delmas-Marsalet).

Casey, Jean-Pierre (2006), *Eligible assets, investment strategies and investor protection in light of modern portfolio theory: Towards a risk-based approach for UCITS*, ECMI Policy Brief No. 2, European Capital Markets Institute, Brussels, September.

CESR (Committee of European Securities Regulators) (2006), CESR's reaction to the reports of the Commission expert groups on market efficiency and on alternative investment funds, CESR/06-461d.

CFA Institute (2005), *Global Investment Performance Standards*.

Clifford Chance (2002), *Constraints on Marketing UCITS Cross-Border in Europe*, Summary Paper, 22 February.

Collins, Andrew, "130/30 Funds – A New Middle Ground", Fortis Prime Fund Solutions (available at www.aima.org).

EFAMA (European Fund and Asset Management Association) and Assogestioni (2005), "Hedge Funds Regulation in Europe: A comparative survey", November.

European Commission (2005), Green Paper on enhancing the EU framework for investment funds, July.

European Commission (2006a), White Paper on enhancing the single market framework for investment funds, November.

European Commission (2006b), Commission Staff Working Document accompanying the White Paper White Paper on Enhancing The Single Market Framework for Investment Funds, Impact Assessment.

European Commission (2006c) Report of the Alternative Investment Expert Group: Managing, Servicing and Marketing Hedge Funds in Europe.

European Commission (2007a), Open hearing on the initial orientations for deepening the single market for UCITS investment funds, Summary report of discussions, April.

European Commission (2007b), Initial Orientations of Possible Adjustments to UCITS Directive (85/611/EEC) Overview of Key Features.

European Commission (2007c), Need for a coherent approach to product transparency and distribution requirements for substitute retail investment products, Call for evidence, 26 October 2007.

European Commission (2007d), Private Placement Regimes in the EU, Call for evidence, April.

European Commission (2007e), Interpretative Communication on the respective powers retained by the Home Member State and the Host Member State in the marketing of UCITS pursuant to Section VIII of the UCITS Directive, Com (2007)112.

European Commission (2008), Investment funds in the European Union: Comparative analysis of use of investment powers, investment outcomes and related risk features in both UCITS and non-harmonised markets, February.

European Parliament (2007), Draft Report on Asset Management II, Committee on Economic and Monetary Affairs, Rapporteur Wolf Klinz, July.

FSA (Financial Services Authority) (2006), *Implementing MiFID's best execution requirements*, DP06/03, May.

INVESCO (2005), *Benefits of an integrated European Fund Management: Cross-border merger of funds, a quick win?*, January.

Kruithof, M. (2005), *Conflicts of Interest in Institutional Asset Management: Is the EU regulatory approach adequate?*, Financial Law Institute, Working Paper Series, WP 2005-07.

La Caixa (2007) "The Spanish economy", Monthly report, December.

Lannoo, Karel (2002), *Pan-European Asset Management*, CEPS Task Force Report, Centre for European Policy Studies, Brussels.

Waters, Dan (2007), "Opening up European markets for fund distribution: The impact of MiFID on UCITS distribution", speech by the Asset Management Sector Leader of the FSA, City & Financial Group Conference, London, 18 January.

Oxera (2006), *Current trends in asset management*, October.

Oxera (2007), *The effect of cross-border investment restrictions on certain pension schemes in the EU*, April.

PriceWaterhouseCooper (2006), *Pan European UCITS Distribution in 2005*.

Socialist Group in the EP (2007), *Hedge Funds and Private Equity: A Critical Analysis*, European Parliament.

ZEW/OEE (Zentrum für Europäische Wirtschaftsforschung/L'Observatoire de l'Epargne Européenne (2006), *Current Trends in the European Asset Management Industry*, Lot 1, October.

ANNEX 1.
STATISTICS ON ASSET MANAGEMENT

Table A.1 Total assets of investment funds, pension funds and insurance companies, 2005 (€ billion and % of GDP)

	GDP	Investment funds	% of GDP	Pension funds	% of GDP	Insurance companies	% of GDP
AT	226.1	156.7	69.3	12	4.7	65.8	29.1
BE	293.1	112.9	38.5	12	4.2	183.8	62.7
DE	2,127.4	965.5	45.4	87	3.9	1,155.6	54.3
ES	641.2	275.1	42.9	90	9.1	173.3	27.0
FI	149.9	44.7	29.8	103	66.1	101.3	67.6
FR	1,550.8	1,270.6	81.9	100	5.8	1,277.7	82.4
GR	193.5	28.3	14.6	n.a.	n.a.	9.2	4.8
IE	155.7	583.3	374.6	78	52.8	78.9	50.7
IT	1,232.8	410.1	33.3	40	2.8	459.5	37.3
LU	25.6	1,525.2	5963.9	105	0.4	n.a.	n.a.
NL	442.8	95.8	21.6	628	124.9	324.9	73.4
PT	127.1	36.4	28.7	19	12.9	40.2	31.6
DK	219.7	106.4	48.4	74	33.6	183.5	83.5
UK	1,890.8	634.6	33.6	1,306	70.1	1,655.2	87.5
SE	303.9	105.6	34.7	44	14.5	288.6	95.0
EU(12)	8,482.9	5,504.6	64.9	1,230	14.5	3,870.3	45.6
EU(25)	11,615.4	6,401.9	55.1	2,583	22.2	6,016.5	51.8
CH	310.7	116.7	37.6	363	117.4	272.3	87.7
US	10,558.5	6,079.0	57.6	10,467	98.9	n.a.	n.a.
JP	3,862.8	441.0	11.4	733	18.8	n.a.	n.a.

Note: EU investment funds data refer to UCITS and non-UCITS products. Data are all 2005 as more recent data for pension funds were not available.

Sources: CEA, Eurostat, EFRP, EFAMA and OECD.

Table A.2 UCITS investment funds asset spread in the EU, June 2007 (€ million and as % of total)

	Total	Equity funds	%	Bonds	%	Hybrid[b]	%	Money	%
AU	118,487	20,364	17.2	52,250	44.1	32,134	27.1	13,739	11.6
BE	121,469	64,694	53.3	10,639	8.8	43,675	36.0	2,461	2.0
DE	281,543	138,308	49.1	66,260	23.5	43,033	15.3	33,942	12.1
ES	283,422	110,467	39.0	121,481	42.9	51,474	18.2	0	0.0
FI	58,332	20,884	35.8	12,930	22.2	6,151	10.5	18,367	31.5
FR	1,473,000	438,200	29.7	198,700	13.5	359,300	24.4	476,800	32.4
GR	23,629	5,993	25.4	5,287	22.4	4,810	20.4	7,539	31.9
IE[a]	654,014	n.a.	n.a.	n.a.	n.a.	n.a.	n.a.	n.a.	n.a.
IT	315,384	66,627	21.1	93,440	29.6	90,056	28.6	65,261	20.7
LU	1,839,131	752,080	40.9	499,452	27.2	342,010	18.6	245,589	13.4
NL	85,677	47,343	55.3	14,131	16.5	22,880	26.7	1,323	1.5
PT	26,295	3,781	14.4	9,732	37.0	4,943	18.8	7,839	29.8
DK	72,787	35,844	49.2	34,977	48.1	1,966	2.7	0	0.0
UK	728,996	494,278	67.8	118,982	16.3	109,868	15.1	5,868	0.8
SE	146,713	102,349	69.8	5,842	4.0	30,233	20.6	8,289	5.6
EU(12)	4,626,369	1,668,741	36.1	1,084,302	23.4	1,000,466	21.6	872,860	18.9
EU(25)	6,309,270	2,324,277	36.8	1,255,151	19.9	1,165,867	18.5	909,961	14.4
CH	120,048	46,555	38.8	25,920	21.6	36,091	30.1	11,483	9.6
US	8,241,701	4,662,800	56.6	1,169,257	14.2	501,860	6.1	1,907,711	23.1

[a] Total of sectoral funds excludes Ireland, for which no breakdown by type of funds is available.

[b] Including balanced funds and funds of funds, except for France and Italy for which the funds of funds data are included in the other fund categories.

Source: Data taken from the EFAMA website.

Table A.3 Asset allocation of insurance companies, 2005 (as a % of total)

	Total[a] (€ million)	Equity[b]	Fixed[c]	Real estate[d]	Others
AT	65,768	44.5	47.1	5.0	3.4
BE	183,797	28.8	68.1	2.1	1.1
CH	272,341	21.1	63.5	8.3	7.1
CY	1,754	26.3	62.5	8.1	3.1
CZ	8,990	12.2	74.3	3.4	10.0
DE	1,155,655	35.9	61.8	2.1	0.3
DK	183,548	35.8	56.1	2.4	5.7
EE	329	24.9	74.8	0.3	0.0
ES	173,322	15.5	63.3	2.9	18.3
FI	101,346	34.9	55.8	9.3	0.0
FR	1,277,679	28.0	66.7	4.0	1.2
GB	1,655,197	49.2	40.0	6.9	3.9
GR	9,267	20.5	40.2	10.4	28.8
IE	78,890	58.5	23.7	7.4	10.5
IT	459,464	14.1	51.4	1.3	33.3
LT	421	1.0	0.0	7.8	91.4
LV	182	10.4	80.2	9.3	0.0
MT	1,233	21.9	62.9	5.1	10.2
NL	324,929	32.0	55.4	4.1	8.6
PT	40,201	12.3	57.7	2.9	27.0
SE	288,588	51.9	44.6	2.7	0.8
SI	3,771	39.6	48.6	4.2	7.6
SK	2,169	14.6	80.1	3.6	1.8
TR	6,233	20.8	62.4	6.3	10.5
EU(25)	6,016,501	36.1	54.1	4.2	5.6
EU(12)	3,870,318	29.4	60.7	3.2	6.6

[a] Total assets include non-life investments.

[b] Variable yield securities and units in investment funds and investments in affiliated undertakings.

[c] Including debt securities and other fixed income securities and loans including loans guaranteed and deposits with credit institutions.

[d] Land, buildings and participating interests.

Source: CEA.

Table A.4 Asset structure of pension funds, 2005 (as a % of total)

	Total[a] (€ million)	Equity[b]	Fixed[c]	Real estate[d]	Mutual funds	Others
AT	11,499	36.5	54.5	1.3	0.0	7.7
BE	12,415	9.8	6.7	1.1	74.9	7.5
DE	86,784	35.1	30.7	3.4	0.0	30.8
DK	521,852	25.9	50.3	1.7	11.2	10.9
ES	90,284	15.2	60.2	3.2	9.0	12.4
FI	102,743	41.3	45.7	7.7	0.0	5.3
FR	99,500	5.3	63.4	3.1	25.8	3.1
UK	1,240,008	40.1	20.2	3.8	18.0	17.8
GR	n.a.	n.a.	n.a.	n.a.	n.a.	n.a.
IE	77,933	65.0	22.0	9.0	0.0	5.0
IT	39,845	9.9	36.5	7.8	11.3	34.5
LU	105	56.4	33.2	0.0	0.0	10.4
NL	627,481	49.8	38.3	3.7	0.0	8.2
PT	18,982	21.1	40.5	8.1	22.1	8.1
SE	386,444	31.0	55.2	3.3	8.0	2.8
EU(12)	1,167,571	40.1	40.9	4.5	4.4	10.2
US	9,935,711	41.3	14.7	0.7	23.5	19.8
CH	344,890	19.8	25.6	9.6	30.2	14.7

[a] Total sectoral funds exclude Greece, for which no breakdown by type of funds is available.

[b] Variable yield securities and units in investment funds and investments in affiliated undertakings.

[c] Including debt securities and other fixed income securities and loans including loans guaranteed and deposits with credit institutions.

[d] Land, buildings and participating interests.

Source: Data from the website of EFRP (www.efrp.org).

Figure A.1 Type of investment funds as % of total net fund assets in EU

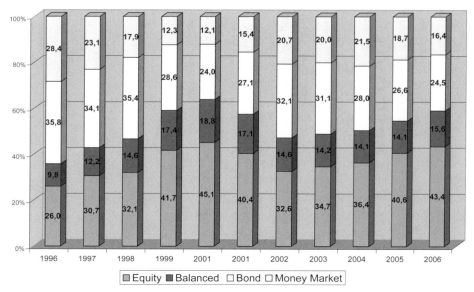

Sources: ICI, EFAMA.

ANNEX 2.
BASIC RULES FOR CAPITAL ADEQUACY & ASSET ALLOCATION UNDER THE EU'S FREE PROVISION OF SERVICES DIRECTIVES

	Capital requirements Directive (Basel II)	3rd Insurance Directives	Pension Funds Directive	MiFID	Investment Funds Directives (UCITS II and III)
Initial capital	Minimum €5 million	Minimum €3 million guarantee fund (€2 million for some classes of non-life insurance)	Where the institution itself underwrites the liability, the rules of the Life Insurance Directive apply	Minimum €125,000, may be reduced to €50,000 for local firms or €25,000 for investment advisers (Directive 2006/49/EC)	Minimum €125,000 plus 0.02% of total assets (as soon as assets exceed €250 million), with maximum of €10 million (UCITS III)
Additional capital requirements	Minimum 8% of risk-weighted assets (Basel Accord) *or* VAR for trading book	Solvency margin must be three times the guarantee fund, and a proportion of technical provisions (in general 4%)	(idem)	Function of trading book (Directive 2006/49/EC)	Capital requirement for position and foreign exchange risk (see annex I Art. 47-56 of Directive 2006/49/EC)
Permissible activities (non-exhaustive, only when related to asset management)	Portfolio management, safekeeping and administration of securities, trading in and underwriting of securities	Life insurance (including group insurance) Non-life insurance (large and mass risk)	Management and investment of funded occupational pension schemes	Individual portfolio management, securities brokerage and order execution activities	Management of investment funds *Non-core:* Individual asset management (including pension funds) Investment advice Safekeeping (custody) and administration of UCITS

Asset allocation	Holdings in non-financial institutions limited to 60% of own funds, and 15% for a single holding. Large credit exposures to single clients are limited to 800% of own funds and 25% for a single exposure.	Harmonised minimum rules: <10% single holding of real estate <5% non-listed securities <10% of assets in single security, except for public debt, and <40% for total large exposures of blocks of 5% <20% in other currency than liabilities	Prudent man rule Member states may set more stringent rules for institutions active on their territory, but within certain limits; Investment in sponsoring undertaking are limited to 5% of the technical provisions	Rules on large exposures	<10% of assets in single security, except for public debt, and <40% for single investments of 5% <10% non-listed securities <10% of same body for money market instruments, and <20% for investments in single other funds and deposits with credit institutions
Conduct of business	Host country rules on advertising and 'general good'	Host country rules on advertising and 'general good' provisions	Host country social and labour rules	Harmonised, but host country in charge of enforcement for branches	Host country conduct of business rules (unless MiFID); Host country advertising and marketing rules
Disclosure	Pillar III	Limited	Disclosure of investment policies, risk and accrued benefits to fund members	Extensive, full price transparency (for equity securities), unbundling of cost of transactions	Simplified and full prospectus (to be updated frequently), half-yearly and annual report
Investor compensation	Deposit Guarantee Directive			Investor Compensation Schemes Directive	Investor compensation schemes (depending upon national implementation)
Final date for implementation	2007-2008	1994	2004	November 2007	August 2003
Technical adaptations	European Banking Committee (EBC), limited	European Insurance and Occupational Pensions Committee, limited	European Insurance and Occupational Pensions Committee, limited	European Securities Committee (ESC), extensive	European Securities Committee (ESC), limited

ANNEX 3.
LIST OF TASK FORCE MEMBERS AND INVITED GUESTS AND SPEAKERS

Chairman: Alain Leclair
Chairman
AFG (French Asset Management Association)

Rapporteurs: Karel Lannoo
Chief Executive Officer &
Senior Research Fellow
CEPS

Jean-Pierre Casey
Manager, Compliance Advisory
Barclays Wealth &
Associate Research Fellow, CEPS

Members of the CEPS Task Force

Ciro Beffi
General Manager
Intesa Sanpaolo

Daniel Bolder
Public Affairs Manager
Deutsche Bank AG

Jean-François Boulier
Chairman Research Committee
Crédit Agricole Asset Management

Jean Echiffre
Managing Director
State Street

Uwe Eiteljoerge (Observer)
DG Markt G-4
European Commission

Florence Fontan
European Affairs
BNP Paribas Securities Services

Fabio Galli
Director General
Assogestioni

Olivier Girard (Observer)
DG Internal Markt
European Commission

Joëlle Hauser
Partner
Kremer Associés &
Clifford Chance

Adrian Hilderly
Investment Managers
Merrill Lynch

Gabriele C. Holstein
Director of European Regulatory
and Industry Affairs
SSBE Ltd London, Zurich branch

Kevin Ironmonger
Head of Compliance, Merrill Lynch
Investment Managers

Stéphane Janin
Director, International Affairs
AFG (Association Française de la
Gestion Financière)

Jean-Louis Laurens
CEO
Robeco France

Mireille Lebrun
Director, Corporate Strategy
Euroclear

Xavier Lucas
AMF

Helmuth Martin
Senior Vice President
Commerzbank EU-Liaison Office
Brussels

Jens Moericke
Market Policy Officer
Deutsche Börse AG

Frédéric Pérard
Head of Global Fund Services BNP
PARIBAS

Lisa Rabbe
Executive Director
Government Affairs
Goldman Sachs International

Wendy Reed
Director
PriceWaterhouseCoopers

Donald Ricketts
Senior Consultant
Head of Financial Services
Fleishman-Hillard Company

Frank Roden
Global Product Head
BNP PARIBAS

Julian Schaub
Executive Assistant
Commerzbank EU-Liaison Office
Brussels

Alastair Sutton
Partner
White & Case LLP

Dominique Valschaerts
Member of the Executive
Committee
Luxembourg Stock Exchange

François Veverka
Executive Vice President
Compagnie de Financement
Financier

Javier Viani
Dpto. de Investigación y Desarrollo
de Producto
Santander Asset Management
Banco Santander

Bernard Wester
Director
Asset Management Fund Service
Credit Suisse

Invited Speakers and Guests

Niall Bohan
Head of Unit - G4
DG Internal Market
European Commission

Anne Bon
Global Head
Legal Teams
AXA-IM

Nathalie Boullefort-Fulconis
Head of Global Sales & Marketing
AXA Investment Managers

Carlo Comporti
Secretary-General
CESR

Mrs. GailLe Coz
Vice President
Head of Industry Affairs
JP Morgan Asset Management

Jean-Baptiste de Franssu
CEO
INVESCO Continental Europe
Services

Vincent Delaunay
Directeur Commercial
Crédit Mutuel – CIC

Tim Grange
Financial Services Authority

Holger Hackländer
Head, Legal & Compliance
COMINVEST

Ashley Kovas
Collective Investment Schemes
Policy
Financial Services Authority

Wolfgang Mansfeld
Member of the Board
Union Asset Management Holding

Raimond Maurer
Chair of Investments, Portfolio-
Management and Pension Finance
Goethe Universität Frankfurt

Maria Dolores Montesinos Trigo
DG Internal Market
European Commission

Sheila Nicoll
Deputy Chief Executive
Investment Management
Association

Arnaud Oseredczuk
Project Chief
Autorité des Marchés Financiers

Michael Schröder
Project Director
Asset Management
Zentrum für Europäische
Wirtschaftsforschung (ZEW)

Rudolf Siebel
Chairman
EFAMA Fund Processing
Standardisation Group

Jarkko Syyrila
Head of European Affairs
Investment Management
Association

Greet T'Jonck
Deputy Director
Commission Bancaire, Financière et
des Assurances